BARBECUE COOKBOOK

THE FINE ART OF OUTDOOR COOKING

Put some more flavor

in your life

PUBLISHER: R. ARTHUR BARRETT
EDITOR: CAROL D. BRENT
ART DIRECTOR: DICK COLLINS
PHOTOGRAPHY BY BILL MILLER

THIS SPECIAL EDITION WAS PREPARED FOR LIGGETT & MYERS INCORPORATED THROUGH THE FACILITIES OF THE BENJAMIN COMPANY, INC., 485 MADISON AVENUE, N.Y.

TESTED RECIPE PUBLISHERS, INC. CHICAGO, ILLINOIS 60648

CONTENTS

REVISED EDITION
SECOND PRINTING APRIL 1972

Library of Congress Catalog Card Number 77-152731

Published in U.S.A. by Tested Recipe Publishers, Inc., 6701 Oakton Street, Chicago, Illinois 60648. Printed in U.S.A. by American Printers and Lithographers, Inc., Chicago, Illinois 60648.

A DIVISION OF JOHN BLAIR & COMPANY

INTRODUCTION

Outdoor barbecues cast a very special kind of happy spell over young and old. No wonder, there's nothing more tantalizing than the sight and smell of food sizzling away on the grill or hibachi, nothing sharpens appetites as quickly. Grilled and spit roasted foods are delicious, easy to fix, fun to eat.

Barbecuing is now a year around thing. Even where the winters are cold and snowy many an avid barbecue chef can frequently be found sneaking out to the garage or breezeway to barbecue a steak or a turkey.

There are scores of plain and fancy charcoal cookers, gas units, electric units and hibachis available, one priced to fit most every budget. Some are small enough to tote to the beach, others are the right size for the apartment terrace or the patio.

The newest cookers and grills are the "gas-fired" and the "electric" ones that can be used the year around. Some require installation and have their own gas (Natural or LP) and electric lines . . . others are mobile and are fired with a fuel such as LP or propane gas or just plug into an outdoor outlet. Both have ceramic briquets, pumice or volcanic rock that heat very quickly and spread even infrared heat over grill area.

This book was developed to make barbecuing easy and fun for both beginner and experienced outdoor chef. It contains all of the information necessary to make those interested a "Master Barbecue Chef." You'll find helpful information about using barbecue equipment, the foods to use, how much to buy and how to prepare favorite and unusual foods on barbecue equipment. And . . . there are hundreds of easy to follow tested recipes for go-with barbecue foods.

To help you select recipes which are different and have a special flair we have placed this seal next to the recipe title *Gourmet* INTERNATIONAL

CHARCOAL BARBECUING

Selecting Equipment

Selecting the proper grill for a beginner is not as easy as it was when all grills looked and cooked very much alike. Now there are many types of grills available using a variety of fuels. They come in many styles, colors and designs; there are good ones priced to fit most every budget even specially designed and built-in ones that cost hundreds of dollars.

It's wise for the beginner to start with a small, inexpensive, portable grill. Use it for several weeks or a season and you'll know whether you're a barbecuing enthusiast or just a sometime outdoor chef. The enthusiast can then make a study of the types of equipment available, weigh the advantages of each and shop around for the unit that does the kind and quantity of barbecuing desired with a minimum of effort. A good hibachi is probably the best place to start.

Save the small experimental grill and use it as an extra grill for heating appetizers, warming breads and desserts, preparing hot dogs and hamburgers in a hurry or toting to the park or beach party.

When Buying a Grill

Purchase a well known brand from a reputable dealer.

Select a well constructed grill with firebox, hood, legs and braces made of heavy duty non-rusting steel or iron to reduce chances of warping, rusting and burning through.

Unit should have a strong heavy duty metal, partial or whole, hood to control wind and save heat.

Be sure all moving parts work smoothly and easily.

On charcoal grills be sure there is a way to control the distance between grill surface and heat or firebox. Grill or firebox must be the type that can be moved up or down easily and quickly to control the heat.

Covered units must have an easy method of adjusting draft over the coals so heat can be controlled.

Grid rods should be heavy and plated with chrome or nickel. They should be closely spaced and flat topped, if possible, to keep small foods from falling through grill and make turning foods easy.

On charcoal units there must be an easy way to add hot coals to fire without disturbing food on grill.

Spit rods should be made of heavy metal and have sturdy forks or prongs. Spit should rotate slowly, clockwise, 6 revolutions per minute (RPM) for proper self-basting.

Spit motor should be listed by Underwriters Laboratories and carry its seal (UL) on the motor to assure safe operation. Motor should have triple prong plug and be used in a properly grounded outlet for safety.

Small Portable Grills

The simplest barbecue grill is a small portable one. There are folding, bucket and brazier-type grills and hibachis . . . all have a small cooking capacity but are easy to use and store. All are completely portable and can be carried to backyard, park, beach or roadside cookout. Here are a few of the more popular small grills:

FOLDING GRILLS: Light, portable and modestly priced. Easy to use, clean, tote and store. These are small fireboxes with grill supported by folding legs when used. Great for beach, roadside or park cookouts.

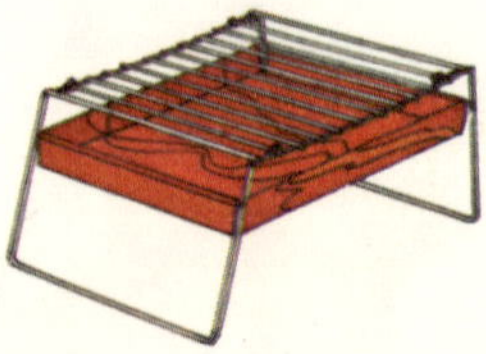

BUCKET GRILLS: Lightweight, portable and inexpensive. A can about the size of a very large pail. Some units have covers which double as a frypan. All styles have a sturdy handle to make carrying easy. All have a removable grill, an inner can for holding charcoal and vent openings at bottom for circulation of air. Fuel can be placed in the inner can before leaving home ready for lighting at the cookout site.

SMALL PORTABLE BRAZIERS: Light, portable and modestly priced. A small version of the big brazier. A round grill 12 to 18 inches in diameter with a firebowl and adjustable grill. Equipped with short or folding legs and available with or without a windshield. Can be used for cooking on table or on ground in patio, park or at beach. The small size and short or folding legs make it easy to transport grill to cookout site.

HIBACHIS: Hibachis are grills borrowed from the Orient and now probably the most "in" of the charcoal grills. They are equipped with adjustable grills, a grate for the charcoal, ashpan, draft door or vents to control the heat.

These fun grills come in a variety of sizes and shapes. Practically all are made of cast iron and are heavy. There are tiny ones 4 to 5 inches in diameter that are fine for heating snacks and appetizers, medium-sized ones fine for barbecuing a steak or two or making an Oriental dinner and big double ones large enough to prepare food for a complete barbecue dinner for 4 to 6. The newest large units have 15 inch square grills and legs to bring the grill up to cooking height. The new hibachis have a removable base for easy removal of ash and for compact storage. The base fits inside the fire box and thus the stored unit takes about one-half the space of the conventional unit. On many units legs can be clamped to the base to bring the grill up to comfortable cooking height.

Hibachis can be used outdoors or indoors when used in fireplace or under an exhaust fan so smoke can be vented to the outdoors. CAUTION—be sure room is well ventilated when you charcoal barbecue indoors as carbon monoxide is tasteless and odorless and deadly poison.

Here are some of the more popular hibachis:

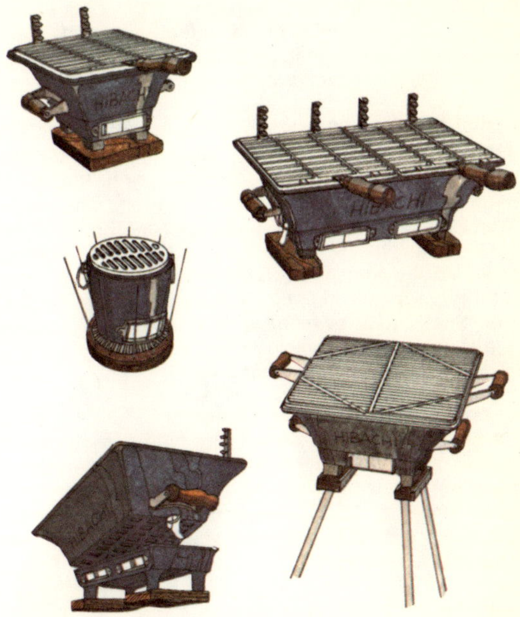

Large Grills and Cookers

LARGE BRAZIERS: The most popular large charcoal grill is probably the brazier with a round heavy duty steel firebowl. The firebowl measuring 12 to 30 inches in diameter is mounted on three or four legs two of which are usually attached to wheels for mobility. Some braziers are equipped with a draft control in the bottom of the firebowl and a crank to regulate the distance between grill and coals to control the heat.

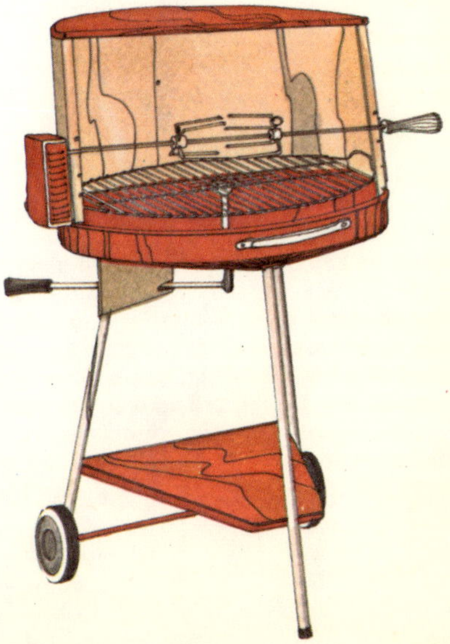

Some braziers have wind screens, half hoods and rotisseries and many even have warming ovens, side tables, etc. All are easy to use, clean and can be taken apart for carrying to park cookout or for winter storage.

Many very fancy, very large versions of the brazier are now available, one of which is mounted on a safety footrail all around and can be used as an outdoor fireplace or cooker or fireplace/cooker combined.

WAGONS AND CARTS: Barbecue wagons and carts are available in a variety of sizes, shapes, features and extras. The simplest wagon is a firebox, grill, full cover and working space mounted on a wagon. The more elaborate wagons are usually made-to-order. Some of the features which can be added are rotisseries, electric charcoal starter, smoke chamber, doors for adding charcoal, storage compartments, shelves, racks and rubber wheels. Some units even have two separate fireboxes and grills making it possible to cook foods at two different temperatures at the same time.

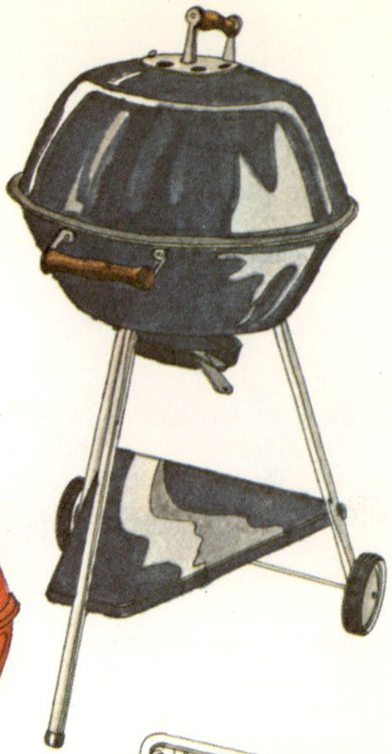

COVERED KETTLES: The large non-rusting all weather porcelain or cast metal covered kettle is a favorite. Popular because a large amount of food can be prepared in it the year round with a minimum of watching and effort and they can be left outdoors all year long. Available in a variety of sizes and colors designed for use on patio, in the recreation room, fireplace, apartment terrace or on a boat.

The deep covered kettle is equipped with grill and charcoal rack. Dampers in bowl and cover make for efficient controlling of heat. Some models have thermometers mounted in the cover, rotisseries, special racks for vegetables, ribs and roasts. All are great for barbecuing food outdoors even on damp, windy and chilly days.

KAMADO—COVERED SMOKE OVEN: This barrel shaped smoke oven is made of heavy heat-proof ceramic or metal to withstand all kinds of weather. It is basically a smoke oven but since it is equipped with a grill, a ceramic or metal bowl for coals and dampers to control heat it may be used for grilling. Most smoke ovens are made to use charcoal and hardwood shavings. Some wood burning smokers are available.

Food is placed on a rack or hung from a hook in the smoke oven and is cooked in the hot smoke. It takes longer to cook food in a smoke oven since low heat and long cooking is necessary to produce the finest smoked flavor.

The smoke oven is unlike any of the other cookers discussed in this book. Important! Study and follow the directions supplied by the equipment manufacturer before using.

CHARCOAL FIRE BUILDING

When do you start? It will take 30 to 40 minutes to build a uniformly hot charcoal fire for grilling or spit barbecuing, so start early!

Experienced barbecuers have their own favorite ways of building a fire. Beginning barbecuers and those with new equipment should follow directions for fire building supplied by the equipment manufacturer. If none is available the following information will be helpful:

WARNING! Never build a charcoal fire or cook on a charcoal grill indoors unless it has its own exhaust and room is well ventilated. A range hood or fireplace can be used. The carbon monoxide given off is dangerous (it is odorless) if confined.

PREPARATION: Line firebowl or box with heavy duty foil, shiny side up, and cleaning will be easier. Punch holes through foil over dampers and vents for proper control of air circulation.

Spread an even layer of gravel, firebase or sand ¾ to 1 inch deep over bottom of firebowl or box so it will give you a level fire base, let fire "breathe," absorb drippings and protect firebowl from overheating and "burning out."

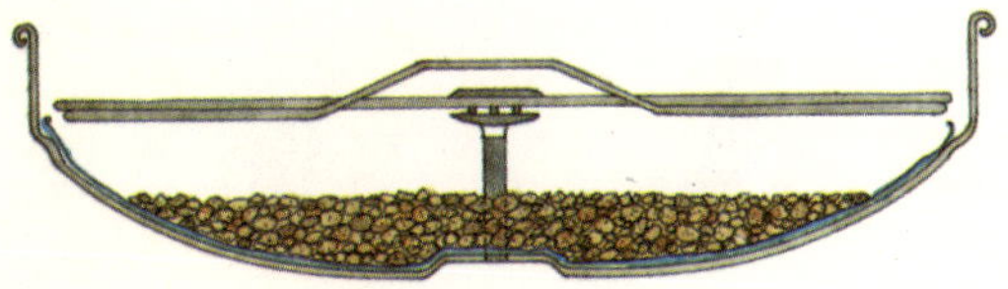

FUEL: Charcoal is available in either lump or briquet. 100% hardwood briquets are preferred by experienced barbecuers. Briquets are uniform in size and give a uniform, intense heat. Lump charcoal ignites quicker than briquets but burns out more quickly. Store charcoal where it will keep dry. If charcoal is damp it will be hard to light.

HOW TO START A CHARCOAL FIRE: Use 25 to 40 briquets depending upon size of grill and length of anticipated cooking time.

The quickest easiest way to start a fire is with one of the starters, either the electric or one of the inflammable liquids, jellies or instant briquets.

LIQUID CHARCOAL STARTER: Use a good safe commercial starter, never make your own and never use gasoline! Pile about 25 briquets in a pyramid in center of prepared firebowl. Drizzle or squirt charcoal starter (about ½ cup) over COLD charcoal. Screw cap onto can of liquid starter IMMEDIATELY after using and put a safe distance away from grill before lighting coals. Drop a lighted match onto charcoal or use a long handled match and light coals in several places.

DANGER! Never add starter to hot or even warm charcoal, it can start a serious fire.

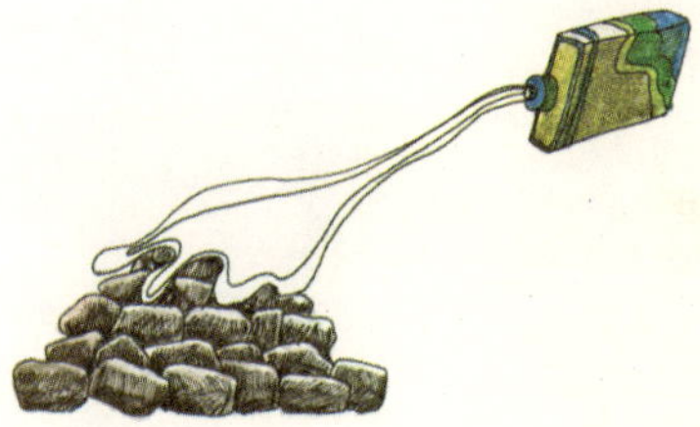

INFLAMMABLE JELLIES: Pile briquets in firebowl as directed for liquid charcoal starter above. Push a small amount of jelly into several crevices in charcoal pile well under briquets using 2 to 4 teaspoons of jelly for about 25 briquets.

PACKS OF TREATED BRIQUETS: Specially treated instant start charcoal briquets packed in cartons are available. These are usually centered in prepared firebowl and ignited. Treated coals can be topped with untreated charcoal before lighting, if a greater quantity of fuel is desired. Light coals at bottom of pile with a long handled match. Treated coals must be completely ignited before placing food on grill or spit or they will impart an unpleasant flavor to the food.

ELECTRIC STARTERS: Some are built into the grill, others are portable. The commonly used portable starter has a long handle with a tubular heating element mounted at one end. The element is placed with a mound or pyramid of charcoal briquets over it in the prepared firebowl or box.

Electricity is switched on and charcoal will heat quickly, in about 10 to 15 minutes. TAKE CARE! The electric starter is very HOT when removed from coals. Place it where there will be no danger of burning people or property while it cools.

COALS ARE READY TO USE WHEN: Charcoal glows (visible in subdued light) and is covered with a thin layer of gray ash. The red glow is hard to see in daylight. Coals covered with a thin layer of gray ash give off an intense and uniform heat. A thick layer of gray ash insulates and smothers coals. Tap coals frequently to loosen ash so fire can breathe.

ARRANGEMENT OF HOT COALS: Depends on the kind of equipment used and food being barbecued.

When barbecuing on grill . . . place gray coals ½ inch apart directly under and covering an area a little larger than the food being barbecued.

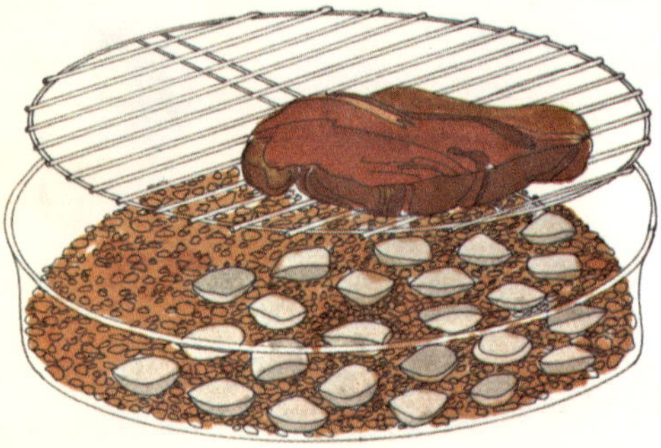

When spit barbecuing on braziers or wagons with hoods or covers pile coals 3 or 4 deep just back of center of roast toward back edge of firebowl and 2 inches beyond each end of roast. If fire is too hot transfer some of the coals to front edge of grill.

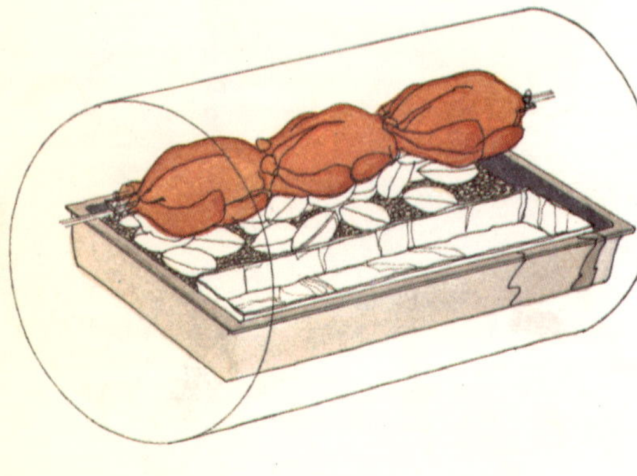

When spit barbecuing in a covered kettle arrange a circle of coals around drip pan placed directly below roast.

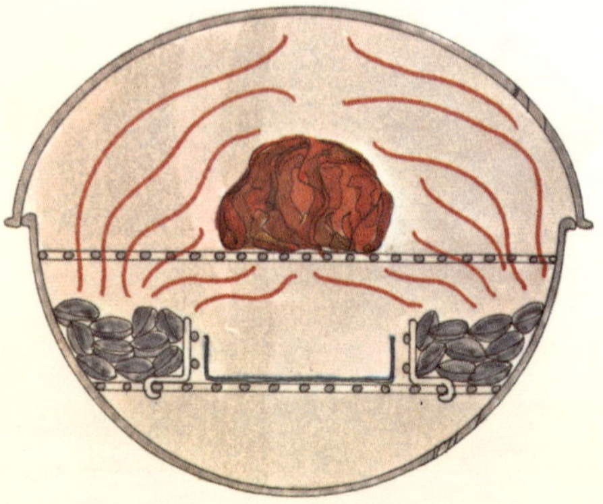

CONTROL OF HEAT: For lower heat . . . Raise grill or lower firebox to increase distance between coals and grill; transfer some of the coals to edge of grill until needed; or, close dampers or draft doors as necessary to control air passing over coals.

For higher heat . . . Lower grill or raise firebox; tap gray ash off of coals; open dampers or draft doors to increase heat; or, add hot coals to fire or warm cold coals around edge of hot coals and then add them to the fire.

TO CONTROL FLARE-UPS: Some grills have built-in flare-up controls. If none is available handle this way.

If meat is very fat remove from grill and trim off excess fat.

If coals can be easily reached separate them with tongs allowing most of fat to drip on gravel or firebase. Don't sprinkle with water as the exploding steam will blow ash onto the food and spoil the taste. Water may also reduce the heat by smothering part of the fire.

TO DOUSE FIRE: Save charcoal when possible for second use. Here are two easy ways. Use tongs and drop hot coals into a large metal pail half full of water to cool. Coals cool almost instantly. Drain and spread charcoal onto paper to dry. Charcoal must be absolutely dry or you will not be able to relight it. Place them in airtight container, or, close dampers and cover firebowl or box with hood or foil to smother fire. When coals are cold transfer them to airtight container. For covered kettles close dampers and coals are ready for use the next time you barbecue.

FACTORS AFFECTING BARBECUING TIME: Intensity of heat as determined by the amount of fuel or heat setting used.

Temperature of food being barbecued—i.e. room temperature (72°F.) or refrigerated temperature (36°F.).

Size of food being barbecued. Large roast or poultry or thick steak or chops take longer than small or thin ones.

Outdoor temperature. Foods cook faster on hot days slower on cold days.

Wind direction and speed. A breeze or a wind dissipates heat on an open unit, less on a hooded unit and even less on a covered unit.

The distance of food from the heat affects barbecuing time. Heat is more intense close to the fire or heat source and reduces as the distance increases.

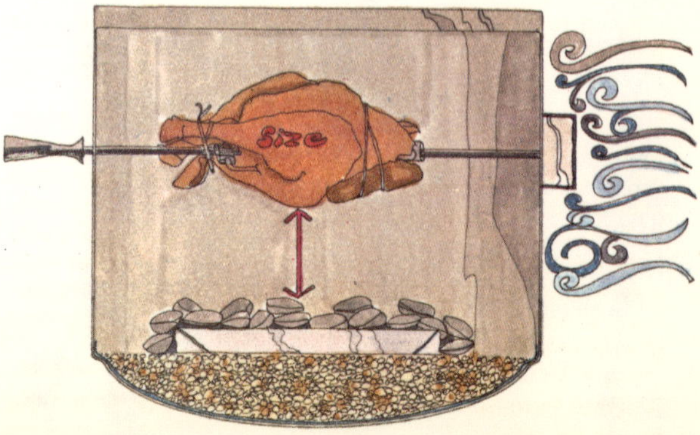

GAS BARBECUING

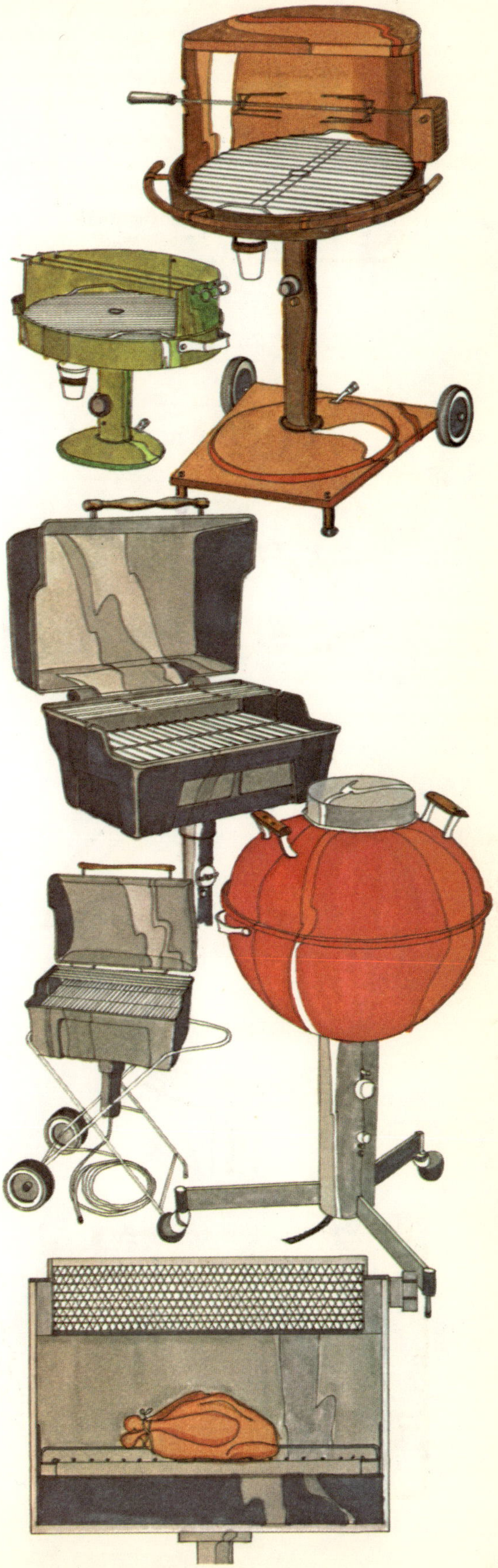

New Gas Grills

The newest barbecue grills are those fired with Natural Gas or LP Gas. Gas grills have many advantages. They cook by RADIANT HEAT, are quick and easy to start and control, cook more quickly than charcoal units, are inexpensive to operate, easy to clean and can be used most any time of the year. Wonderful too for installing indoors for they do not require the ventilating needed for charcoal units.

Gas grills are either rectangular and box-like in shape, spherical like a covered kettle or circular with a sturdy wraparound towel bar. These latter look like the conventional charcoal brazier. Some of these units can be mounted on a post in the ground or on a patio base or cart. Others are on wheels. Units mounted on pedestal or post can usually be rotated to provide wind protection without disturbing the fire. The trend seems to be away from the stationary post type unit to the semi-movable or wheeled type units.

Permanently installed grills generally use piped in natural gas or LP. Portable gas grills use LP Gas (propane, butane, etc.) which comes in tanks and is piped through a flexible hose or copper tube coupled to the grill. Semi-portable units are movable and generally plug into gas service by means of a hose with a quick disconnect fitting. With the new designs and improvements in installation methods it is many times faster and more economical to use an LP installation rather than plumb in natural gas. Many units are available for either natural or LP Gas and some come with two orifices one for each type of gas.

Important! Gas grills are still new to many and differ greatly from grill to grill. Directions for using each may also vary. Know your grill before using it. Read all use and care information supplied by the manufacturer of your gas grill before using it. Unfortunately most manufacturers include little or no information so we have tried to fill this gap. A few general directions follow:

Gas grills are available in a wide range of styles, sizes and prices. Units are available for every size family and are priced to fit most every budget. There are small ones with single burners and grills, with or without covers, and very large, very fancy double ones with lots of built-in accessories. Larger units include warming shelves, windshields, storage cabinets, motorized rotisseries, rotisserie baskets and drip pans. Cost varies with the size of grill and the "extras."

A safety feature . . . burner knobs on all gas grills lock or can be removed.

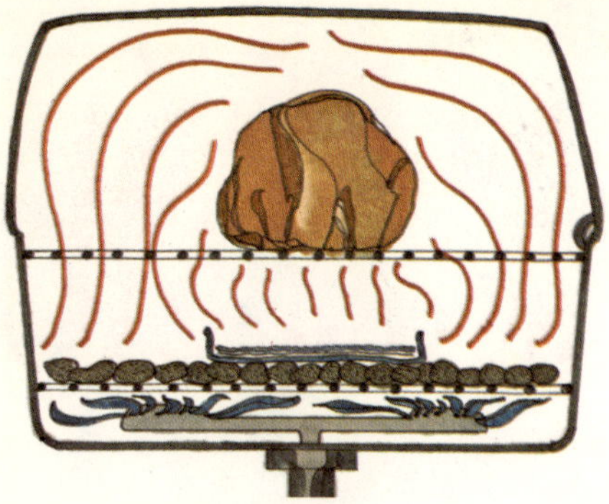

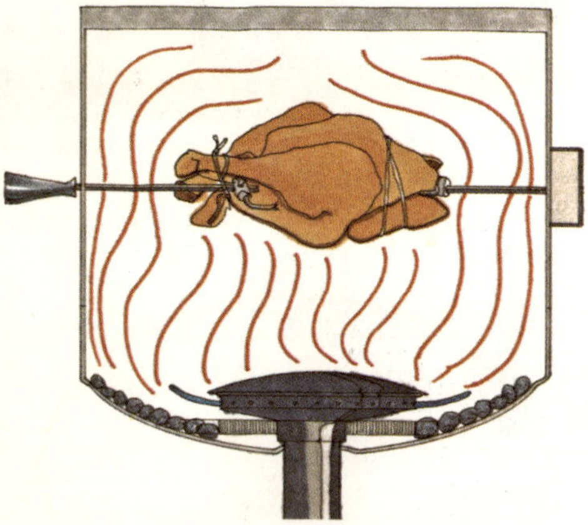

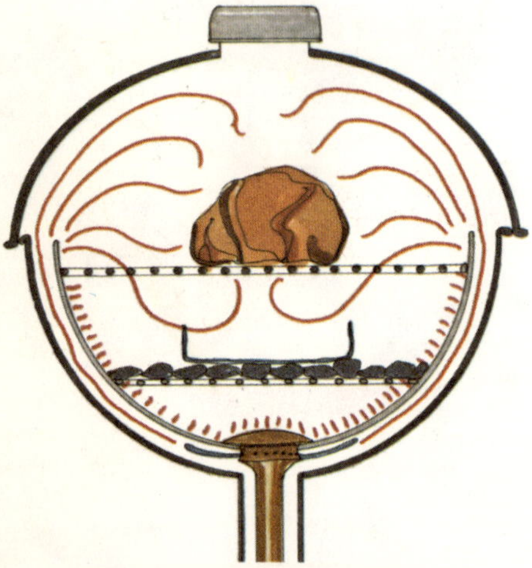

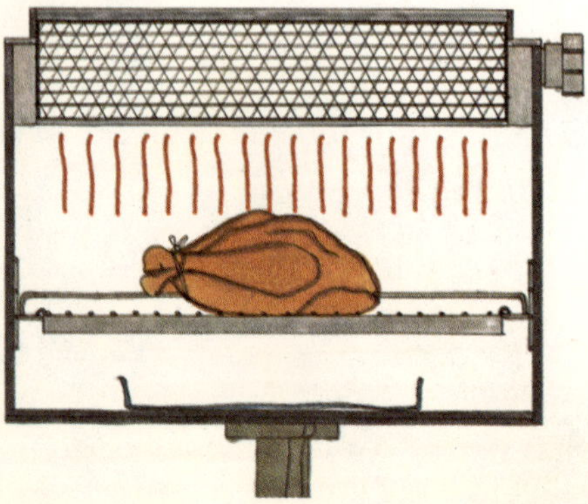

Gas Grills Are Fun

HOW TO USE: When unit is installed, have lowest temperature set to maintain 300°F. with cover closed.

Raise hood or cover and remove grill. Grill should always be removed when preheating unit as the intense heat of the **HIGH** setting can warp and ruin the cooking grill in a very short period of time.

Strike long handled match or light a soda straw; be sure cover is open, push in and turn handle of gas valve to **HIGH** and ignite gas through lighter opening. If you are fortunate and have an electric or spark igniter follow manufacturers directions. Preheat 5 to 10 minutes when burner is below food, 1 minute when burner is above food, and 3 to 5 minutes when burner is above rocks but below the food. When you are barbecuing a roast or large piece of meat or poultry it is not necessary to preheat unit. Preheating is primarily for grilling or broiling as a good even blanket of infrared heat is desirable.

Heat for barbecuing is supplied by "Infrared Radiation" from the top above the food or from below the food depending upon location of burner. The burners heat the almost indestructible self-cleaning ceramic block, briquets or volcanic rocks which in turn give off infrared heat which barbecues the foods.

As a general rule for spit barbecung use **MEDIUM-HIGH** position for rare or quick cooking foods, **MEDIUM** for medium rare foods and **LOW** for well done or foods requiring long slow cooking.

Discourage flame ups. When hot fat drips onto ceramic rocks or briquets smoking results. In small amounts this is not objectionable. Remember no amount of burning juice or fat is going to give charcoal flavor. If smoke is too heavy move food to another section of grill, rotate grill or reduce heat.

When a special smoky flavor is desired scatter hickory, cherry, apple or hardwood chips, soaked in water for about one-half hour, over briquets.

Most gas grill manufacturers do not recommend the use of drip pans. On most enclosed or covered units you can save the juices for gravy or for basting. Place a rack or trivet in the bottom of a drip pan or metal roasting pan. Place pan in center of cooking grill and then place roast or poultry on rack. Foods barbecued in this manner are cooked by the indirect method. See drawing page 11.

Some manufacturers recommend placing the drip pan directly on the ceramic rocks or briquets under the food on the spit or on the grill (indirect method). A small amount of water must be added to the pan to keep juices from boiling away and the heat must be reduced.

Turn burner to OFF position when barbecuing is completed. If you are using LP or tank type fuel turn fuel off at tank when not in use.

DRIP PANS

When charcoal barbecuing meat or poultry on spit or in a covered cooker on the grill a drip pan should be used. Catch the drippings and fat for making gravy or for basting food during barbecuing.

Aluminum foil drip pans are easy to make with heavy duty aluminum foil, see directions below.

A metal drip pan can be substituted for a foil one. They are usually available where barbecue equipment is sold. Aluminum foilware pans can also be used when barbecuing on the grill.

TO MAKE A DRIP PAN: Use 18-inch heavy duty aluminum foil. Tear off a sheet of foil the length or diameter of the grill or 5 inches longer than meat being barbecued on spit or grill.

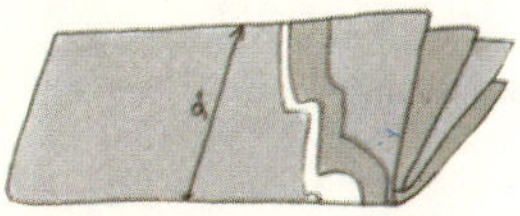

Fold foil exactly in half lengthwise.

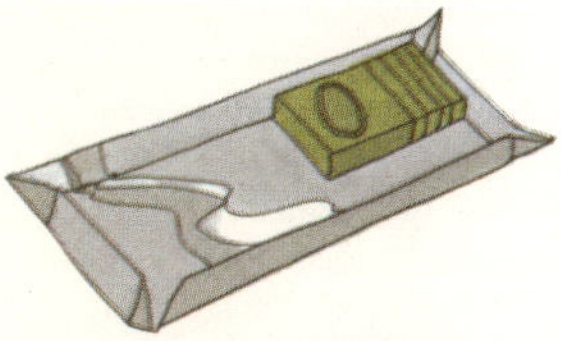

Fold an edge 1½ inches high on all 4 sides of foil. Use a wooden cutting board or cardboard box to make firm sharp corners. Pull corners out from sides as shown.

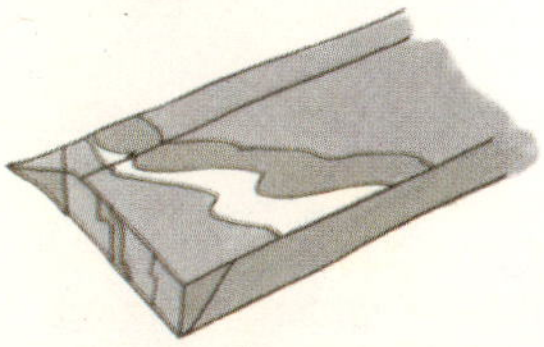

Remove board or box from foil tray; miter corners.

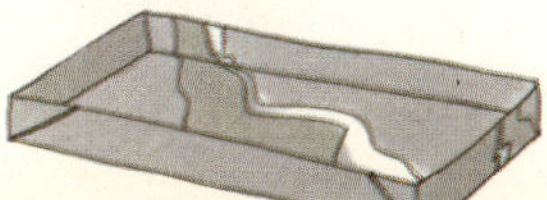

Fold corners back firmly against sides to make seams smooth. Pinch corners together to make pan rigid.

How To Place A Drip Pan

CHARCOAL UNITS: When used under spit on charcoal grill set drip pan level and parallel to and slightly in front of spit rod and directly on gravel, firebase or fire grid.

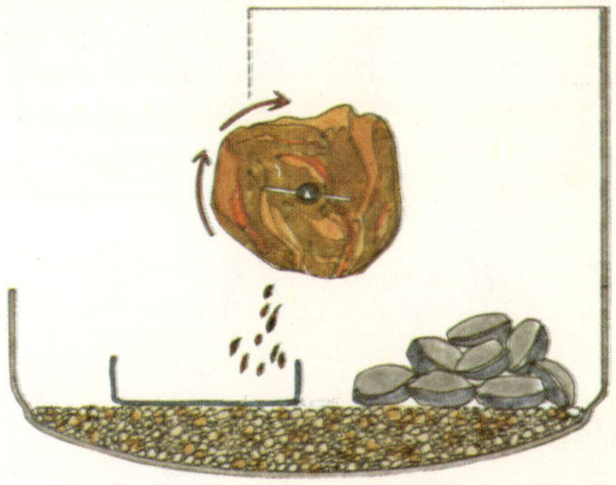

When used under grill on covered cooker or kettle place pan flat and level on fire grid directly under food being barbecued.

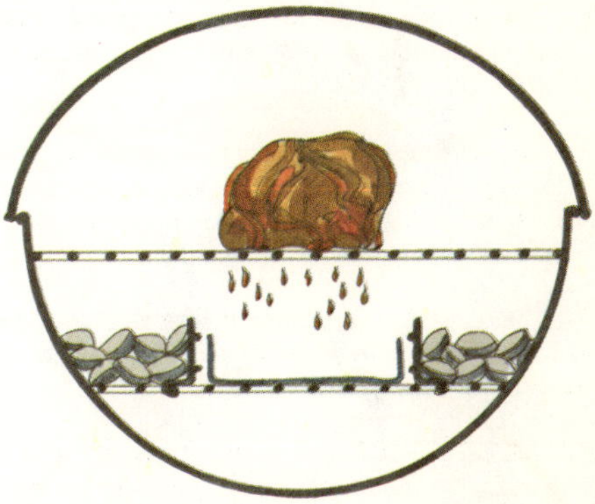

For braziers, wagons and carts arrange fire before placing drip pan. For covered cookers or kettles place drip pan before starting fire.

Make sure drip pan does not rest on burning coals. Empty drip pan carefully when ⅓ to ½ full.

GAS UNITS: Follow instructions on this page for making a drip pan and instructions on page 10 for placing drip pan on gas units.

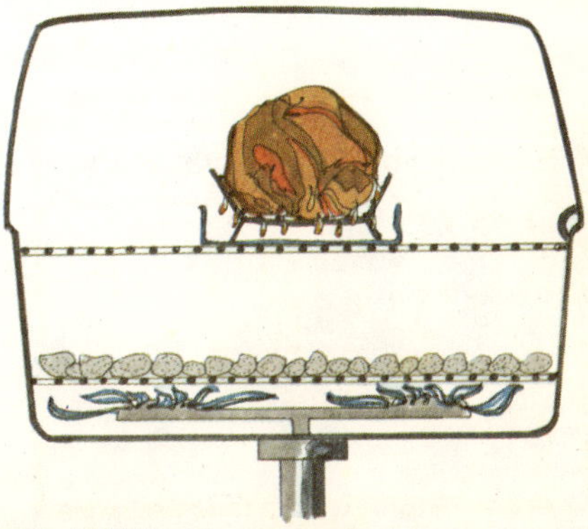

ELECTRIC UNITS: Most manufacturers recommend a foil lining on bottom of unit.

ACCESSORIES

Only a few tools are needed in addition to a good grill to barbecue a steak or prepare a tempting dinner over an open fire. Outdoor barbecuing is easier when tools designed for a particular task are available. The market is stocked with an endless number of gadgets; some are basic tools everyone should have, others nice to own and use, many are extravagant or worthless gadgets.

The Basic Tools and Supplies

FUEL: Charcoal briquets, lump charcoal, liquid fuel, gas or electricity. Check fuel recommendations given in the instruction folder supplied by manufacturer of the barbecue equipment being used.

GLOVES: Work gloves to handle unlighted charcoal, fuel or grill; asbestos gloves with long gauntlets and pot holders to prevent burns.

GRAVEL OR FIRE BASE: To form a base in charcoal units for coals to protect bottom and allow for better circulation of air or as directed by equipment manufacturer.

FIRE STARTER: Matches, electric fire starter, charcoal lighter fluid, inflammable jelly or pretreated charcoal in special packs.

LONG HANDLED TOOLS: Fork, wide spatula and 2 pair of tongs, one for handling hot coals, another for handling food.

FIRE EXTINGUISHING MATERIAL: Fire extinguisher, water and/or sand.

WORK SURFACE: Table near grill.

CONTAINERS: Refuse pail, large paper sacks.

Accessories, Practical, Convenient

ALUMINUM FOIL: Heavy duty 18-inch foil for lining fire box, wrapping foods, etc.

FIRE RAKE: To level or move gravel, fire base or charcoal.

ROTISSERIE ASSEMBLY: Motor, spit and forks.

EXTENSION CORD: Extra long, heavy duty, three pronged, grounded, waterproof cord to attach to fuel starter or rotisserie motor.

PLIERS: To tighten scews on rotisserie spit prongs.

SPIT BASKET: To fill and attach to spit for barbecuing. Baskets excellent for poultry, steaks, chops, fish, seafood. The constant turning bastes foods while barbecuing. They are great for spareribs, chicken halves or parts, chops, shrimp, etc.

OTHER TOOLS: Sharp knives for cutting, boning and carving meat, slicing breads, vegetables and fruits.

SALT AND PEPPER SHAKERS: Long handled ones are not much use.

THERMOMETERS: A meat or barbecue one to indicate internal temperature of roast. See specific recipe for directions for inserting thermometer tip. Grill and spit level thermometers to indicate temperature at grill or at spit level.

BASTING BRUSHES: Two or 3 sizes. Be sure to have long handled brush for basting roasts and steaks and medium sized ones for kabobs, fish and desserts.

HINGED BROILERS: Long handled ones, excellent for handling small portions of food which could fall through grids on grill or be time consuming to turn such as shrimp, chicken livers, small chicken pieces, hot dogs, appetizers, etc. Ideal, too, for cooking food which becomes fragile during cooking such as fish fillets or patties, very thin hamburger patties, etc. Great for toasting bread and rolls, too.

SPECIAL HOLDERS: Designed for whole fish, franks, burgers and roasts.

BRACE FOR POULTRY: Makes tying or trussing unneccessary.

VEGETABLE RACKS: Fit around edge of grill; excellent for baking potatoes.

SKEWERS AND SKEWER RACK: Select 6-inch, 8 to 10-inch, and extra long metal skewers. Most practical long ones come with rack, or have double prongs which keep foods from sliding during cooking. Bamboo skewers of varying lengths are great for appetizer or dessert kabobs or Oriental style entrées. Soak bamboo skewers thoroughly in water before using to reduce charring.

STIFF METAL BRUSH: With or without scraper to clean grill.

PANS: Long handled heavy frypan and pancake griddle, others for sauces.

COFFEE POT.

BRANDING IRONS: Just for fun. Purchase ones with initials of the host or ones that indicate whether steak is rare, medium or well-done.

TABLE TOTER: Basket or cart to store away, to bring out and transport plates, cups, napkins, paper towels, knives, forks, spoons, tablecloth, etc. to serving area. You may want to include platters, salad bowls, servers, trays, ice bucket, vacuum jug or pitcher.

COVER: Plastic or canvas to protect grill when not in use.

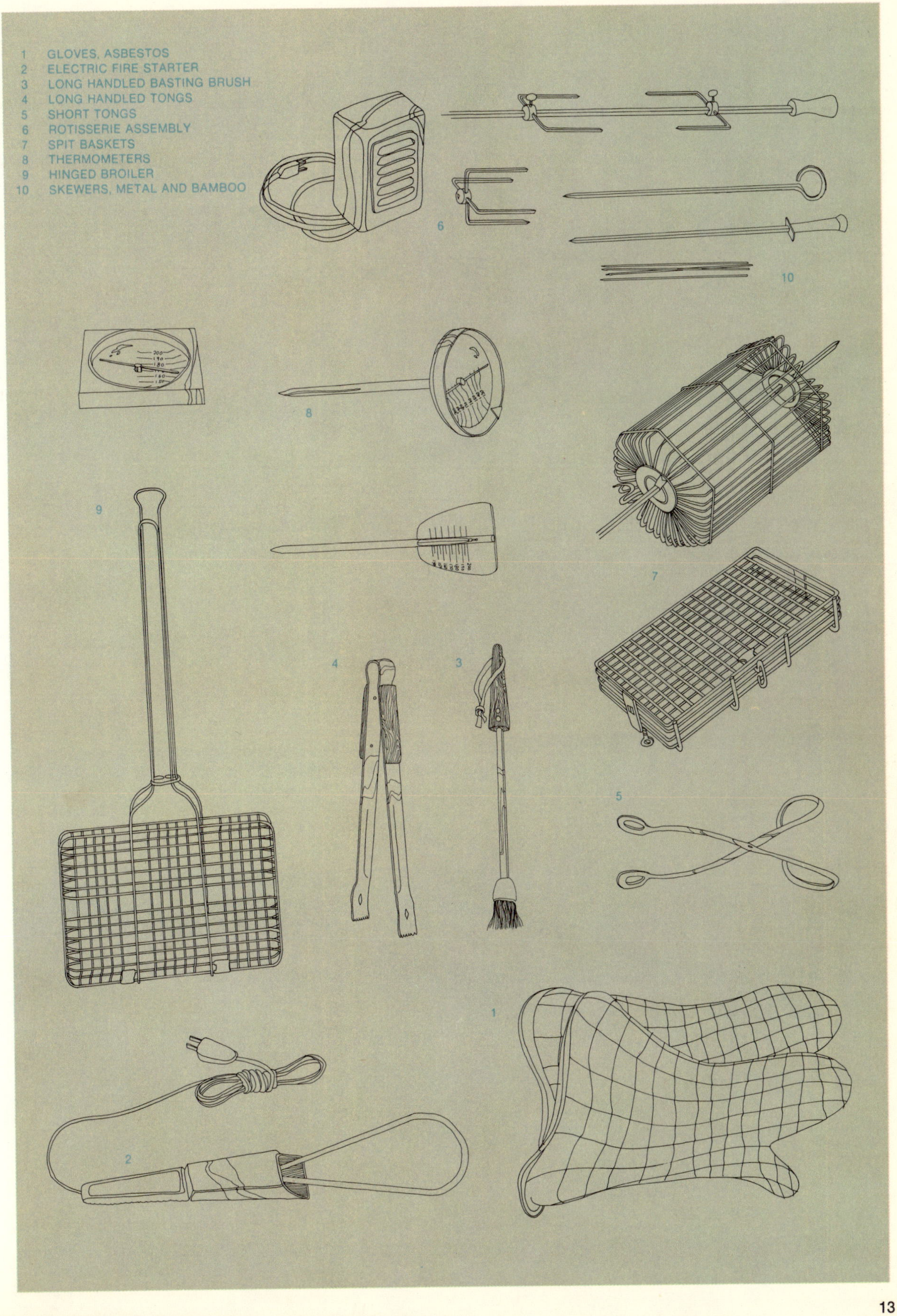
1 GLOVES, ASBESTOS
2 ELECTRIC FIRE STARTER
3 LONG HANDLED BASTING BRUSH
4 LONG HANDLED TONGS
5 SHORT TONGS
6 ROTISSERIE ASSEMBLY
7 SPIT BASKETS
8 THERMOMETERS
9 HINGED BROILER
10 SKEWERS, METAL AND BAMBOO

TRICKS

Spit Roast Meats, Fish and Poultry

See specific directions for spit roasting meats, fish and poultry on pages listed below:

BEEF	
Standing and Boneless	20-22
LAMB	
Leg of	29
PORK	
Ham, bone-in and boneless	31
Loin, bone-in and boneless	30
Spareribs	33
FISH	37-38
POULTRY	
Chickens	41
Duckling	42
Rock Cornish Hens	43
Turkey	44-45

Estimate Temperature Without A Thermometer

WHEN NO MEAT THERMOMETER IS AVAILABLE: Judge grill or spit barbecue level temperature (as directed below) and barbecue or spit roast for time suggested in cook chart in specific food section.

ESTIMATE TEMPERATURE AT GRILL LEVEL: Hold hand cautiously, palm side down, just above grill and judge temperature by number of seconds hand can be kept in position. Count seconds this way.

1000—1
1000—2. . . **HIGH** or Hot
1000—3. . . **MEDIUM-HIGH** or Medium Hot
1000—4. . . **MEDIUM**
1000—5. . . **LOW**

These temperatures are used in the recipes in this book and are shown in **BOLD** type. These same temperatures approximate the dial markings on most gas grills.

ESTIMATE TEMPERATURE AT SPIT LEVEL: Hold hand cautiously palm side down just below roast on spit and proceed as for grill level above.

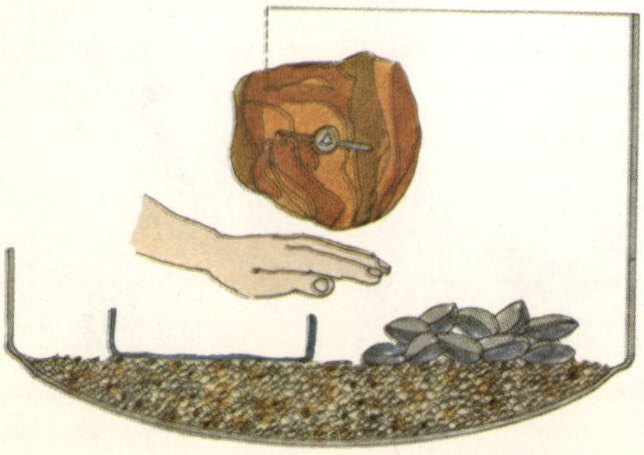

How To Use A Barbecue Meat Thermometer

Select a quality make meat thermometer specially designed for roasting meat and turkey. Thermometer should be a sturdy metal one with a sharp pointed tip. If spit barbecuing, make sure thermometer does not touch top of barbecue hood or coals when turning. Proceed as suggested below:

POULTRY: Insert tip of thermometer into thickest part of thigh close to body or in heaviest part of breast. Make sure tip is away from bone.

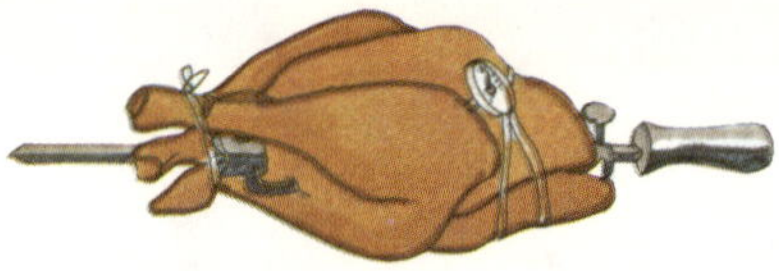

BONELESS ROLLED ROASTS: (Beef, Pork, Ham, Turkey, etc.) Insert shaft of thermometer into roast at a slight angle so tip rests in center of thickest part of roast away from fat pockets and spit, if used.

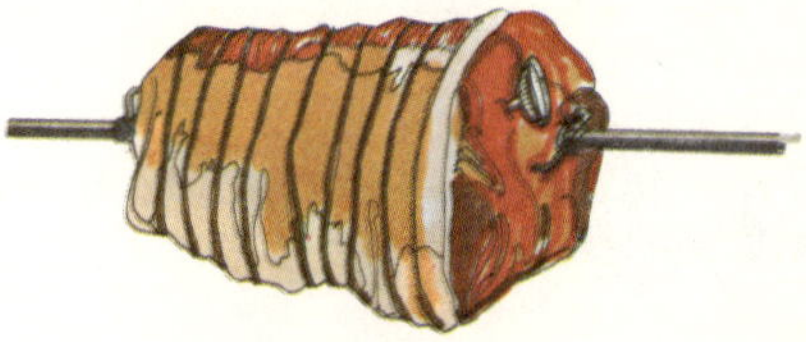

BONE-IN STANDING BEEF RIB ROAST OR PORK LOIN: Insert shaft into roast at an angle with tip in center of roast and at thickest part of meat away from bone, fat pocket or spit, if used.

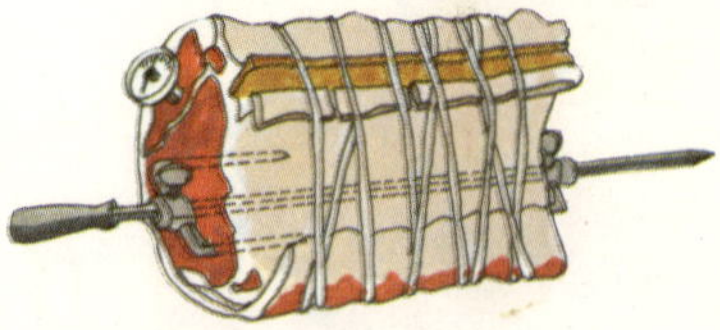

BONE-IN HAM OR LEG OF LAMB: Insert shaft of thermometer at an angle with tip in thickest part of butt end of ham or leg of lamb, away from bone, fat pocket or spit, if used.

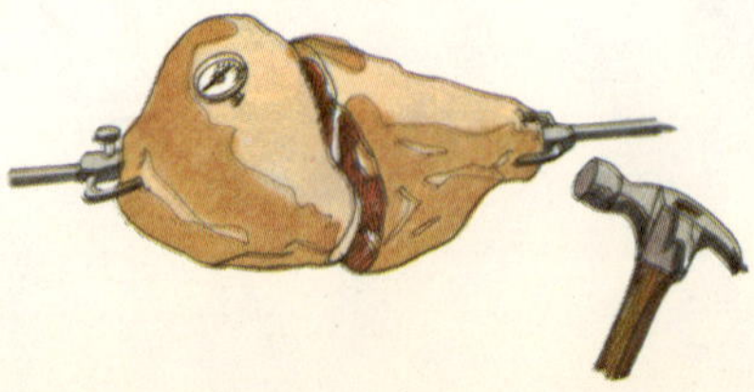

Care and Safekeeping of Barbecue Grills

Keeping barbecue equipment in good condition is fairly simple. Just a little time and work at the right time keeps the barbecue grill looking new, in good working condition and extends its life.

Some barbecuers with an eye on the easy chair argue that cleaning the grill is unnecessary since the flames of the next fire sterilize everything. All equipment should be cleaned after each use and it's easiest to clean it right after using.

IMPORTANT! Read the cleaning, care and storage directions supplied by the manufacturer of your equipment before using any cleaning products, chemicals or abrasives.

CLEANING CHARCOAL BARBECUE EQUIPMENT: Before starting fire dust or wipe off grill, grid, hood, etc. Line firebowl or box completely with heavy duty foil (see drawing on page 7) before spreading gravel or firebase. Arrange coals and drip pan as directed on page 8 to minimize spattering and flame ups. Before putting food onto grill brush it lightly with cooking oil or rub with a piece of fat cut from meat. Oiling will help to keep foods from sticking to grill making it easier to clean off burned on food and fats.

RIGHT AFTER BARBECUING: Put on asbestos mitts; remove hot grill and clean in one of these ways:

If grill is small enough, plunge it into hot sudsy water in a service sink; forget it until you have time to clean it.

Or, with asbestos gloved hand, wipe off top and bottom of hot grill with cold wet cloth. The cold water will turn to steam and remove soil.

If grill is large, soak 2 thick stacks of newspapers (12 to 14 sheets each) on cement or gravel surface using hose. Place hot grill on one stack of soaked papers; cover with second. Hose down papers; let stand 30 minutes. Burned on food will usually wash off easily with a wet cloth, cellulose sponge or stiff grill brush.

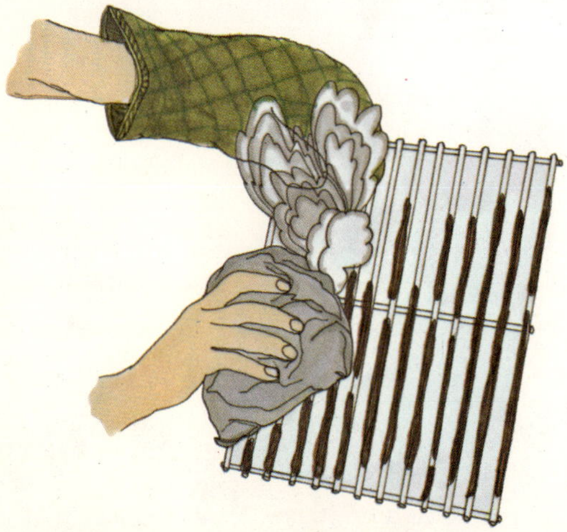

To clean firebowl or box douse fire and save charcoal (see page 8). Gather up edges of foil and fold over gravel or firebase. Press edges together into neat package; save for second use or discard if messy. Gravel can be washed and dried for further use. Wipe cooled firebowl with damp cloth; dry.

BEFORE STORING: Oil axles on wheels and mechanism for raising and lowering grill. Rub grill lightly with cooking oil. Reassemble; cover and store in clean, dry place.

CLEANING GAS GRILLS: IMPORTANT! Gas grills vary considerably so it is very important directions for cleaning equipment supplied by manufacturer of equipment be followed exactly.

TO CLEAN GRILL: Follow directions for charcoal barbecue equipment (this page).

TO CLEAN BRIQUETS: Gas grills with ceramic or volcanic briquets or rocks below the grill burn off about 90% of the drippings as the food cooks. As soon as the grill is removed after barbecuing partially close barbecue grill and turn heat to **HIGH** position. Briquets or rocks will clean themselves in about 10 minutes. When briquets or rocks darken on one side turn them over and residue will burn off the next time the grill is used. Where ceramic block is above the grill it is completely self-cleaning.

TO CLEAN BURNERS: If burner is below food. Use a stiff brush to remove any burned-on particles. Use a wire brush to open clogged ports or holes.

If burner is above food. Burner is practically self-cleaning because the intense infrared heat burns off most particles as the food cooks. After each use, cool and spot clean so grease will not build up.

EXTERIOR: Follow directions supplied by manufacturer. If none are available, cool unit, wash with hot sudsy water, rinse well and dry.

STORAGE: Reassemble when clean and dry; cover and store in clean, dry place.

BEEF

For sheer elegance, easy preparation and superb eating, nothing tops barbecued beef. Even the ordinary hamburger takes on a new exciting flavor. Steaks barbecued on the open grill have no equal and are probably America's favorite meat.

Today there are many modestly priced beef roasts available designed for spit roasting and barbecuing. Beef rump, eye of the round and chuck roasts make wonderfully fine roasts and are moderately priced. Being the less tender cuts they require long slow or moist cooking.

Steak . . . Always a Sizzling Success!

Steak, crispy on the outside, juicy pink on the inside, is probably the favorite food of most Americans. No meat is more tempting sizzling on the grill or more satisfying eating than steak. And . . . there's a steak for broiling on the hibachi or grill priced to fit most every budget! So to be a good Steak Chef know your steaks and how to cook them.

Be a Good Steak Chef

Steaks vary in grade, size, tenderness and price. They come boneless and with the bone in. Some are exceptionally tender while others are less tender but when properly prepared are tender, elegant, economical eating.

Choose beef that is firm, has a fine-grained texture, a bright cherry-red color, well-marbled with thin streaks of creamy white fat and has a coating of firm flaky fat around the edge. Buy the best grade of steak possible, those stamped U.S. Prime, Choice or Good or quality branded ones. You will find a U.S. Prime or Choice grade chuck steak, properly prepared, is often more tender, better eating and less costly than a U.S. Good grade sirloin steak. Learn to recognize these steaks by their shape and bone; they are considered the best steaks for broiling on the grill.

Steak Cuts

PORTERHOUSE: Sometimes called large T-Bone, is one of the finest steaks. It has a T-shaped bone and contains a generous section of tenderloin. Steak for several, depending upon thickness.

T-BONE: Very like porterhouse except is smaller in size and has a smaller section of tenderloin. Usually a single serving.

STRIP: A tender cut from the top loin, available boneless or with bone in. Sometimes called a Kansas City steak or New York cut. Usually a single serving.

SIRLOIN: Pin, flat or wedge-boned steaks are cut from the loin; probably the most popular steak for broiling on the grill. All cuts are tender, ideal for serving several.

RIB EYE: The eye of the rib, sometimes called a Delmonico or Spencer steak. Extra lean; deliciously tender, usually a single serving.

CLUB: Cut from the small end of the loin. A tender steak, usually a single serving.

FILET MIGNON AND CHATEAUBRIAND: Cut from the tenderloin. Center cuts are used for chateaubriand, the ends for filet mignon. Both are extremely tender, the most expensive steak cuts.

RIB: Cut from the first 3 ribs. Modestly priced, comes boneless or bone in. Usually a single serving.

CHUCK: Top quality blade or 7-bone steaks, fine for broiling on the grill, usually without tenderizer. Round-bone chuck steaks when tenderized with a marinade or commercial meat tenderizer make inexpensive delicious steaks, great for serving a crowd.

ROUND: Top, bottom or full round steaks are ideal for serving a crowd inexpensively. Tenderize with marinade or commercial meat tenderizer as desired.

FLANK: Top grade (Prime or Choice) flank steak is used for London Broil. This beef, quickly broiled to the rare stage and sliced very thin diagonally across the grain is inexpensive excellent eating.

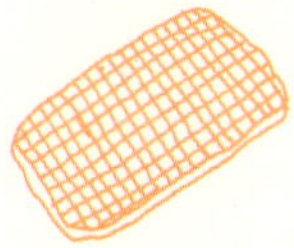

MINUTE OR CUBE STEAKS AND HAMBURGERS: These economical meats are not true steaks. See pages 24 to 27 for preparation and cooking directions of these grill favorites.

How Much Steak To Buy

WEIGHT	
BONE-IN STEAKS	. . . Allow ¾ to 1 pound of raw meat per adult serving.
BONELESS STEAKS	. . . Allow ½ pound of raw meat per adult serving.
THICKNESS	
PORTERHOUSE TENDERLOIN SIRLOIN	. . . 1½ to 2 inch
T-BONE STRIP CLUB ROUND	. . . 1 to 2 inches
CHUCK	. . . 1½ to 3 inches
FLANK	. . . Whole

Prepare Steak for Barbecuing

Trim excess fat from outer edge of steak to reduce flame ups. Save suet for greasing grill.

To prevent steak from curling make shallow cuts around fat edge of steak about 1½ inches apart. Take care! Don't cut into the lean meat, meat juices will escape! Thick steaks don't require this slashing.

Marinate tender steaks for flavor. Use a commercial meat tenderizer or marinade to tenderize the less tender cuts. Follow directions for use of tenderizer supplied by manufacturer.

◀ *Fillet Mignon*

Broil Steaks on Grill

Start charcoal fire about 45 minutes ahead of time, as directed on page 7, so there will be a uniform heat. Preheat gas grill as the manufacturer of the equipment recommends or as suggested on page 10.

Rub grill or hinged broiler, with suet or brush with cooking oil.

Thermometers are available to place on grill to indicate heat available at grill level.

APPROXIMATE TEMPERATURE AT GRILL LEVEL	
HIGH	400 to 425°F.
MEDIUM-HIGH	375°F.
MEDIUM	350°F.
LOW	325°F.

Place large steaks on grill about 5 inches above **MEDIUM** to **HIGH** heat, thin steaks about 4 inches above **HIGH** heat. If a charred surface is desired or you wish to sear steaks place them 2 to 3 inches above heat for the first 2 or 3 minutes of cooking. Adjust grill to the proper cooking height and finish cooking first side. Repeat process for second side.

On gas units with fixed position grills turn heat to **HIGH** for the searing process and then turn to **MEDIUM** and finish the cooking. See chart for approximate broiling time on page 19.

Turn steaks just once! Turn when the meat juices start to bubble up through the meat to the top of the steak; see time chart on page 19.

Use tongs to turn steak. Plunging fork tines into meat causes juices to escape. If it's absolutely necessary to use a fork plunge tines into a fat section of the steak.

Brush steak with favorite basting sauce or marinade (see recipes on pages 56 to 59) several times during cooking; season with salt and pepper just before serving or after each turning, as desired.

Keep an eagle eye on the steaks while they're cooking. Take steaks off the grill the minute they're done and serve immediately. See chart for approximate cooking time on page 19.

Want a Special Flavor?

SMOKY FLAVOR: Cover for the last few minutes of broiling time with grill cover or sheet of aluminum foil.

HICKORY FLAVOR: Sprinkle dampened hickory chips or sawdust on charcoal briquets or rocks on gas grills a few minutes before steaks are done; cover as directed above for stronger flavor.

CHAR FLAVOR: When cooking each side, lower grill close to heat source (2 or 3 inches) or turn gas to **HIGH** for 2 or 3 minutes of cooking then raise grill or lower the gas to **MEDIUM** and cook as directed in recipe.

Check for Doneness

Make a small slash in center of steak with the point of a sharp knife and examine inside color of steak. Rare steak is red, medium is pink and well done is gray. A steak will cook a bit after removal from grill so stop broiling when steak tests slightly pinker than desired. Continue cooking if steak is too rare.

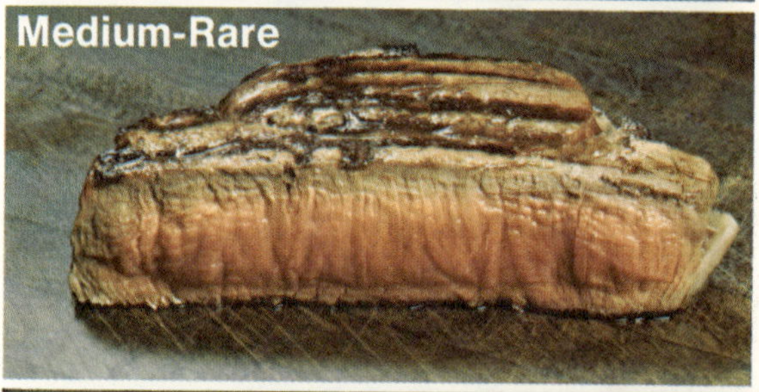

Carving Large Steaks

PORTERHOUSE AND SIRLOIN: Carve steak so each serving will include an equal amount of the very tender and less tender meat.

Place cooked steak on wooden cutting board. Using a very sharp pointed knife, cut all around and very close to the bone. Remove bone and push meat pieces together. Cut into 1 inch slices across the width of the steak or in thin diagonal slices for sandwiches as indicated below.

CHUCK, ROUND AND FLANK: Place cooked steak on wooden cutting board. Remove bone as directed above. Use a sharp carving knife and fork and slice very thin *on the diagonal across the grain of the meat!*

Barbecuing Time For Steaks

CUT	THICKNESS (Inches)	RECOMMENDED HEAT* GRILL LEVEL CHARCOAL	SETTING GAS	APPROXIMATE BROILING TIME PER SIDE (Minutes) RARE	MEDIUM	WELL-DONE
TENDER STEAKS (Porterhouse, T-Bone, Tenderloin, Sirloin, Rib, Rib Eye and Club)	1	**HIGH**	**MEDIUM-HIGH**	4-6	6-8	9-11
	1½	**HIGH**	**MEDIUM-HIGH**	5-7	9-11	11-15
	2	**MEDIUM**	**MEDIUM to MEDIUM-LOW**	7-10	14-18	18-22
FLANK (London broil and others)	Whole (1½ to 2 pounds)	**HIGH**	**MEDIUM-HIGH to MEDIUM**	4-7	Not recommended	
CHUCK (round or blade bone), marinated or tenderized	1½	**HIGH**	**MEDIUM to MEDIUM-LOW**	5-7	9-10	Not recommended
	2	**HIGH**	**MEDIUM to MEDIUM-LOW**	8-10	14-17	Not recommended
	3	**MEDIUM**	**MEDIUM-LOW**	20-25	30-40	Not recommended
ROUND marinated or tenderized	1	**HIGH**	**MEDIUM-HIGH**	4-6	6-8	Not recommended

*For gas units preheat for 5 minutes. It is better to have the heat too low rather than too high. For charcoal see page 14 to determine how to measure heat at grill level.

Steak au Poivre *(Pepper Steak)*

Gourmet INTERNATIONAL™

Select a 4 to 5 pound sirloin steak 1½ inches thick. Rub and press 2 teaspoons cracked or coarsely ground whole black pepper into each side of steak using the palm of the hand. Let stand at room temperature 1 to 1¼ hours. Broil on hibachi or grill as directed on page 18 to doneness desired over **MEDIUM** to **MEDIUM-HIGH** heat, see chart for approximate cooking time on this page. Transfer steak to heated flameproof platter. Sprinkle with salt. When steak is about done sauté ½ cup sliced onions in heavy frypan in 1 tablespoon butter or Onion Butter (see page 58). Spoon onions onto steak. Top with a few overlapping thin tomato slices. The true gourmet will warm ¼ cup brandy or cognac; ignite and spoon over steak. When flame dies, bone and slice steak across the grain. Yield: About 6 to 8 servings.

Family Barbecue Steak

Marinate favorite steaks (large or individual) in favorite marinade (see page 59). Broil as directed on page 18. Baste with Southwestern Barbecue Sauce (see page 56) during barbecuing. Serve with remaining sauce.

Steak with Mushrooms

While favorite large steak is broiling on grill, sauté ½ pound small washed mushrooms in 3 tablespoons butter or margarine until tender. Season with salt and pepper. Serve on steak with Bearnaise Sauce (see page 56).

Roquefort Cheese Steak

Gourmet INTERNATIONAL™

Mash 1 small clove garlic. Add ¼ cup softened butter or margarine and ¾ cup crumbled Roquefort cheese; mix well. Spread over hot broiled sirloin, porterhouse or other large steak the last 2 or 3 minutes of broiling.

Sherry-Soy Steak

Gourmet INTERNATIONAL™

Place a Prime, Choice or tenderized good grade steak 1 to 2 inches thick in shallow dish. Pour Chinese Marinade over meat (see page 59). Cover; refrigerate 1 to 4 hours, turning steak several times. Drain steak; prepare as directed for steaks (see page 18). Brush steak with leftover marinade several times during barbecuing. Serve plain or with Curry Butter or Basting Sauce (see page 58). Yield: 4 to 6 servings.

Salt Broiled Steak

Gourmet INTERNATIONAL™

Select a lean boneless 3 to 5 pound tender steak, about 2 inches thick. Moisten coarse (not rock) salt with enough water to make a thick paste. Spread one side of steak with a ½ inch layer of salt. Cover with a double thickness of dampened paper towel or brown paper; turn and repeat process on second side. Broil about 5 inches above **MEDIUM** heat about 15 minutes per side. When steak is done, remove paper and scrape off salt. A hinged broiler is handy for this operation. Serve with Garlic Butter (see page 58). Yield: About 6 to 8 servings.

London Broil

Gourmet INTERNATIONAL™

Score a Prime or Choice grade flank steak (about 1½ pounds) with sharp knife on top and bottom of steak making cuts about ¼ inch deep. If desired marinate steak (see page 59) or use a commercial meat tenderizer as manufacturer directs. Broil to rare stage on greased grill. See page 18 for cooking directions. Never broil flank steaks to well-done stage; the meat will be very tough. Brush meat with melted butter, favorite marinade of basting sauce (see page 59) several times during cooking. Season as desired with salt and pepper. Carve as directed on page 18. Yield: 4 to 6 servings.

Beef Roast

A large juicy roast turning on the open spit or barbecued in a covered unit is everyones favorite. Cooked slowly over a **MEDIUM** heat it does not dry out and can be done to the degree you wish.

Tender Beef Cuts

STANDING RIB ROAST: Bone-in. Tender meat on rib bones; covered with a layer of white fat. Lean well marbled with fat, fine meat to serve a crowd. Roasting requires little attention, serving is easy and it's liked by most everyone.

Have meat man cut off shortribs, back cord and chine bone; prepackaged meat usually has these removed.

Select a 2 to 7 rib roast weighing 4 to 20 pounds, depending upon needs.

ROLLED RIB ROAST: Same as standing rib roast except meat is boned, rolled and tied. Easy to balance on a spit, roast, carve and serve; very little waste. A 2-rib roast usually makes a 4 to 6 pound rolled roast.

RIB EYE, SPENCER OR DELMONICO ROAST: Boneless and tied; tender eye muscle of the rib. Delicious meat, easy to balance on spit, roast, carve and serve; little waste.

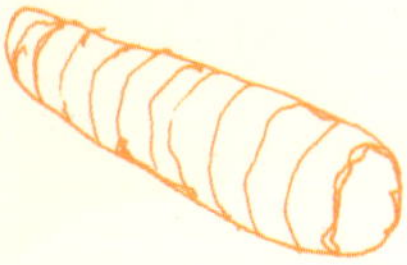

TENDERLOIN: Boneless. Most expensive and most tender of all beef roasts. Very lean, delicate flavor, little waste. Whole tenderloins weigh 5 to 8 pounds and can be cut into 2 or 3 small roasts.

SIRLOIN TIP: Boneless. Sometimes called top sirloin, sirloin roast or butt. May be rolled, covered with fat and tied. Flavor excellent.

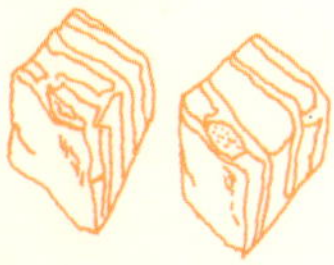

SHORT RIBS: Cut from end of standing rib roasts; vary from 2½ to 4 inches in length, cut 1 to 2 ribs wide. Bones large; small amount of meat on each rib. Cook in spit basket, on grill or in covered cooker.

Less Tender Beef Cuts

EYE OF ROUND: Boneless, covered with fat and tied. May be tenderized with commercial tenderizer or in tenderizing marinade. Fine flavored meat, economical. Important! For finest eating slice meat very thin and diagonally across the grain of the meat.

STANDING OR ROLLED RUMP: Boneless. Select only top grade (Prime or Choice). If it's a standing rump, have meat man trim the meat well, roll and tie it into a compact piece. If roast is not covered with fat it will need frequent brushings with cooking oil or a butter basting sauce during barbecuing to keep surface moist. Excellent flavor, little waste, slices easily, economical.

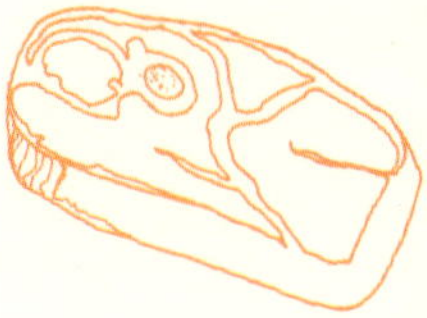

CHUCK OR ROUND: Bone-in. Select only top grade meat (Prime or Choice). Have roast cut 2½ to 3 inches thick. May be tenderized with commercial meat tenderizer or in a tenderizing marinade. Cook in covered cooker or on grill as directed for a Chuck Steak (see page 19).

What to Buy*

CUT	ALLOWANCE PER SERVING (Raw Weight)
BONE-IN ROASTS	½ to ¾ pound
BONELESS ROASTS	⅓ to ½ pound
SHORT RIBS	¾ to 1 pound

*When barbecuing select a large roast, enough for two meals. The larger roast usually cooks better with less loss per pound and leftovers can be quickly turned into delicious entrées with fresh-cooked goodness.

How to Cook

Beef may be barbecued on the spit, in covered cooker or directly on the hibachi or grill.

Beef Cuts in Covered Cooker

Read directions for barbecuing beef supplied by manufacturer of equipment being used or follow these general directions:

Place roast, fat side up, directly on cooking grill over drip pan or on rack in shallow pan in preheated gas or charcoal covered cooker. (See page 11 for placement of drip pan and heating cooker.) Barbecue over **LOW** to **MEDIUM** heat (325 to 350°F.) at grill level. See page 14 for way to estimate temperature if no grill thermometer is available. Cover; barbecue for 1½ hours with dampers open. Insert barbecue or meat thermometer tip into center of thickest part of roast away from bone and fat pocket. Cover; continue barbecuing until meat is doneness desired, 140°F. for rare, 160°F. for medium, 170°F. for well-done. See approximate Barbecuing Time For Beef page 22.

Baste meat occasionally with drippings or oil while barbecuing. Brush with favorite barbecue sauce (see recipes page 56) 3 or 4 times during last 30 minutes of barbecuing, if desired. Allow to cool 15 to 20 minutes before carving.

◀ *Beef Roast, Rolled and Standing*

Beef Cuts on Rotisserie Spit

The size and weight of a roast being barbecued on spit is limited by the length and sturdiness of the spit and the power of the motor. When properly balanced even a light weight spit and motor can handle a large roast.

Read directions for spit barbecuing supplied by the manufacturer of the equipment being used or follow these general directions:

Meat man usually ties boneless cuts of meat. Tie bone-in cuts with heavy string or butcher's cord, if possible. See drawings below for tying standing rib roasts. If you can't get roast prepared in this manner try to get a roast where ribs are cut to 7 inches.

Slip one prong or fork onto spit, points away from handle. Push spit lengthwise through center of meat so it is as nearly as possible balanced on spit. Slide second prong or fork onto spit, points towards meat. Push prongs into meat.

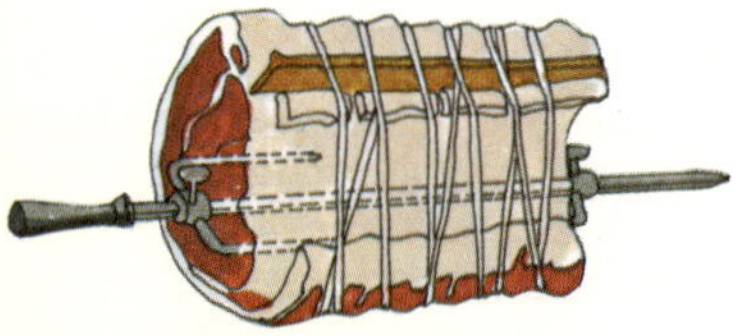

Test spit for balance. Roll spit back and forth on palms of hands. If it turns smoothly it is well balanced. Readjust spit in meat if necessary. Tighten prong screws with pliers. Insert barbecue or meat thermometer tip at a slight angle (to keep it from falling out) into center of thickest part of roast away from spit, bone and fat pockets.

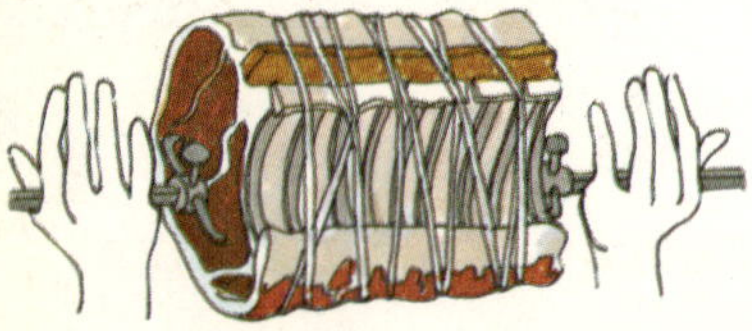

Attach spit to motor of preheated unit. Make sure thermometer will not hit top of cooker, grill or coals when turning. See page 11 for information about drip pans, heat or distribution of coals, etc.

Spit level temperature for barbecuing most beef should be **LOW** to **MEDIUM** (325 to 350°F.). If no spit level thermometer is available gauge temperature at spit level this way. Hold hand cautiously, palm side down, under roast and count seconds this way, 1000—1, 1000—2 is **HIGH**, 1000—3 is **MEDIUM-HIGH**, 1000—4 is **MEDIUM** and 1000—5 is **LOW.** For covered gas type units set at **LOW** to **MEDIUM-LOW**, and for open hood units set at **MEDIUM.**

Barbecue meat until it is fork tender and has reached the doneness desired, internal temperature of 140°F. for rare, 160°F. for medium or 170°F. for well-done. Brush meat 3 or 4 times during last 30 minutes of barbecuing with favorite barbecue sauce (see recipes page 56), if desired. Cool 15 to 20 minutes before carving.

Barbecuing Time For Beef Roast

CUT	WEIGHT (Lbs.)	COOK TO INTERNAL TEMPERATURE (°F.)*	APPROX. MINUTES PER POUND	GRILL OR SPIT TEMPERATURE DEGREES OR SETTING
STANDING RIB	6-8	140°	22-24	325°-350°F.
		160°	27-30	**LOW to**
		170°	32-35	**MEDIUM**
ROLLED RIB	6-8	140°	28-32	325°-350°F.
		160°	32-36	**LOW to**
		170°	38-45	**MEDIUM**
TENDERLOIN				
WHOLE	4-6	140°	12-15	350°-375°F.
		160°	15-18	**MEDIUM to MEDIUM-HIGH**
HALF	2-3	140°	20-25	
		160°	24-28	
RIB EYE	4-6	140°	18-20	325°-350°F.
		160°	20-23	**LOW to**
		170°	22-25	**MEDIUM**
SIRLOIN TIP	4-6	140°	20-25	325°-350°F.
		160°	23-27	**LOW to**
		170°	28-32	**MEDIUM**
CHUCK or ROUND	4-6	170°	25-30	325°-350°F. **LOW to MEDIUM**
ROLLED RUMP	4-6	160°	22-25	325°-350°F.
		170°	25-30	**LOW to MEDIUM**

*140°F.—rare
160°F.—medium
170°F.—well-done

Oriental-Style Barbecued Short Ribs

Gourmet INTERNATIONAL™

Trim excess fat from 4 pounds of beef short ribs. Arrange in large shallow dish. Pour Chinese Marinade (see page 59) over ribs; cover and refrigerate 2 to 3 hours. Drain ribs; save marinade. Arrange ribs, bone side down, on hibachi or grill, 5 to 6 inches above **LOW** to **MEDIUM** heat (325°F. to 350°F.). Cover with cooker cover. Cook with dampers open until almost tender, 1 to 1¼ hours, brushing frequently with marinade. Remove cover; cook until ribs are fork tender and evenly browned, turning as needed to brown evenly. Serve with Chinese Barbecue Sauce (see page 56). Yield: About 4 servings.

Spit Roasted Short Ribs

Place 5 pounds of top grade beef short ribs in large shallow dish. Pour Sherry Soy Marinade (see page 59) over ribs; turn and cover. Refrigerate 2 to 3 hours, turning ribs 2 to 4 times. Drain ribs; save marinade. Place ribs in greased spit basket leaving space between each rib. Close basket; attach to rotisserie spit. Start fire (see page 7) or preheat unit (page 10). Attach to motor and switch motor on. Barbecue over **MEDIUM** heat (350°F.) at spit level until ribs are fork tender and brown, about 2 hours. Baste with reserved marinade during the last 30 minutes of barbecuing. Serve with Barbecue or Southwestern Barbecue Sauce (see page 56). Yield: About 6 servings.

Chuck Roast in Spit Basket

Sprinkle amount of instant nonseasoned meat tenderizer over a 2 inch thick chuck roast (4½ to 5 pounds) and treat as manufacturer of tenderizer suggests on label. Place in well greased spit basket; close tightly. Attach basket to spit and spit to motor. Start motor and barbecue over **LOW** to **MEDIUM** (325°-350°F.) at spit level until fork tender. See Approximate Time, Temperature and Setting Chart page 22. Baste with oil or melted butter or margarine during barbecuing. Brush with favorite barbecue sauce (see recipes page 56) 3 to 4 times during last 25 minutes of cooking. Yield: About 8 servings.

Beef Tenderloin on Grill

Carefully trim excess fat from surface of tenderloin. Tie string or butchers' cord around the meat at 1½ inch intervals. Place directly on well greased **HIGH** (425°F.) hibachi or grill 4 to 6 inches from heat source. See page 14 for way to estimate temperature if no grill thermometer is available. Cook meat to doneness desired, 140°F. for rare, 160°F. for medium. See Approximate Time, Temperature and Setting Chart page 19. Baste meat often with melted butter or margarine during barbecuing. Serve rare for best flavor.

TENDERLOIN ROAST ON THE SPIT: Follow preparation directions above but place on spit as directed on page 22. Allow slightly longer cooking time. When the thick part of the roast is rare the center is medium and the end well-done.

Corned Beef Roast

Simmer a 3 or 4 pound corned beef brisket as directed on package label. Drain and pat dry with paper towels. Combine and mix ½ cup light brown sugar, ½ teaspoon each of cloves, dry mustard and ginger. Rub roast with sugar-spice mixture. Fasten securely in spit basket. Cook over **LOW** to **MEDIUM-LOW** heat 4 to 5 inches from heat source 1 to 1¼ hours. Serve with favorite Barbecue Sauce, see page 56, if desired. Yield: About 8 servings.

Beef Tenderloin on Grill

Great Ways with Hamburgers, Minute and Cube Steaks

The classic hamburger is about as American as baseball and apple pie. The cooking is easy and few foods are better than the lowly burger or more exciting eating when served with interesting toppings and fine flavored sauces.

What To Buy

Freshly ground lean beef chuck, round or sirloin tip all make great hamburgers. Even freshly ground hamburger meat or ground beef purchased at top quality meat departments will make excellent hamburgers. Select freshly ground chuck or sirloin tip if the hamburgers are to be thick or rare.

How Much To Buy?

Dinner-size burgers ....1 pound will serve 2 or 3

Burgers to serve in buns ......1 pound will serve 3 to 4

Double burgers ...1 pound will serve 3 or 4 (6-8 patties)

To Prepare Hamburger Patties

Select one of the basic hamburger recipes on pages 24 to 27. Mix ingredients carefully and shape meat into thin or thick patties without packing meat together.

To Broil Hamburgers on Grill

Lightly grease hibachi, grill or hinged broiler. Arrange patties on grill or, if available, in hinged grill and close. Broil on **MEDIUM-HIGH** grill about 4 inches above heat to doneness desired, turning patties only once. See chart page 25 for approximate broiling time. Brush patties with marinade, melted butter or favorite basting sauce (see recipes on pages 56 to 59) 2 or 3 times during broiling.

To Broil Minute or Cube Steaks

Marinate minute or cube steaks 30 minutes before broiling (see recipes on page 59), if desired. Drain well; place on greased hibachi or grill. Broil on a **MEDIUM-HIGH** grill 2 to 3 inches over heat until well browned on both sides, turning steaks once. See chart on page 25 for broiling time. Serve with favorite barbecue sauce (see recipes on page 56). These inexpensive steaks make great sandwiches on French bread or in hamburger buns or onion rolls.

Barbecuing Time and Heat for Hamburgers, Minute and Cube Steaks

CUT	THICKNESS (Inches)	RECOMMENDED HEAT GRILL LEVEL CHARCOAL	RECOMMENDED HEAT SETTING GAS	APPROXIMATE BARBECUING TIME PER SIDE (Minutes) RARE	MEDIUM	WELL-DONE
HAMBURGERS	½ to ¾	425°F.	MEDIUM-HIGH	3-4	4-6	6-8
	1	425°F.	MEDIUM-HIGH	4-5	6-7	8-10
MINUTE OR CUBE STEAKS	¼ to ½	425°F.	MEDIUM-HIGH	1½	2	2-4

Beefsteak Burgers

2 pounds ground lean beef chuck, round, sirloin tip or hamburger meat
¼ cup finely chopped onion
1 egg
2 teaspoons Worcestershire sauce
2 teaspoons salt
⅛ teaspoon pepper
Butter or margarine or favorite basting sauce (see pages 57 to 59)

Combine and mix ingredients except butter, margarine or basting sauce. Shape into 6 or 8 patties ¾ inch thick. Arrange on tray; cover and refrigerate until ready to cook. To broil, arrange patties on hot well-greased hibachi, grill or on hinged broiler about 4 inches above heat until crusty brown on underside; turn and cook to doneness desired. See chart on page 25 for broiling time. Baste patties with melted butter or margarine or basting sauce several times during barbecuing. Serve on favorite hamburger buns. Yield: 6 or 8 burgers.

Dinner-Size Beefsteak Burgers

Follow recipe for Beefsteak Burgers, above, except shape meat into 4 or 6 patties 1 inch thick; broil 5 inches above heat. See chart on page 25 for barbecuing time. Yield: 4 or 6 servings.

Penny-Saver Burgers

Follow recipe for Beefsteak Burgers (above) and change meat mixture as follows. Reduce meat to 1½ pounds ground beef and add ½ cup uncooked rolled oats and ⅓ cup tomato juice or milk. Yield: 6 or 8 burgers.

Dinner-Size Penny-Saver Burgers

Follow recipe for Penny-Saver Burgers (this page); shape meat into 4 or 6 patties 1 inch thick. Yield: 4-6 servings.

Steak Burgers

2 pounds ground lean beef chuck, round or sirloin tip
¼ cup finely chopped onion, optional
2 teaspoons salt
⅛ teaspoon pepper
Butter or margarine or favorite basting sauce (see pages 57 to 59)

Combine meat, onion, salt and pepper; mix. Shape into 6 or 8 patties ½ to ¾ inch thick. Broil as directed for Beefsteak Burgers (this page). Serve on favorite hamburger buns. Yield: 6 to 8 servings.

Dinner-Size Steak Burgers

Follow recipe for Steak Burgers (this page) except shape meat into 4 or 6 patties 1 inch thick. Broil 5 inches above heat. See chart above for broiling time. Yield: 4 or 6 servings.

Freeze-Ahead Burgers

Shape 2 pounds ground beef chuck, round or sirloin tip into 4, 6 or 8 patties. Place each on a square of waxed paper on a baking sheet; freeze. Transfer frozen patties to plastic freezer bag. Label and store in freezer until 30 minutes before cooking time. Remove waxed paper and broil as directed for Beefsteak Burgers (this page) except season with salt and pepper after the first turning and after removing from grill. Yield: 4 dinner-size or 6 or 8 sandwich-size burgers.

For Galley or Camp Stove Cooking

Any of the above hamburgers can be broiled in a portable electric broiler, cooked in a hot frypan or broiled in a galley stove equipped with a broiler, if desired.

Burgers with Fancy Toppers

Variations

Follow Beefsteak, Steak or Penny-Saver Burger recipe (above) and change or serve as follows:

ALOHA BURGERS: Shape meat into 4 dinner-size patties. Baste burgers during broiling with melted butter or margarine. Brush hot burgers with Curry Sauce (see page 56) and top each with a pair of hot grilled pineapple slices and a wedge of avocado. Garnish with watercress or mint, if desired. Serve with Curry Sauce. Yield: 4 dinner-size servings.

BACON BURGERS: Shape meat into 6 or 8 patties. Combine and mix ½ cup dairy sour cream and 2 tablespoons finely chopped green onion. Wrap two bacon strips around each patty; secure with wooden picks. Top each cooked burger with a dollop of sour cream mixture and garnish with 2 or 3 tomato wedges. Yield: 6 or 8 dinner-size servings.

CHEESEBURGERS: Two or three minutes before removing favorite hamburgers from grill top each with a slice of processed American cheese and let cheese soften. Serve on toasted hamburger buns.

BLUE CHEESE BURGERS: Follow recipe for Pocket Burgers (see page 27); substitute small pieces of blue cheese for American or Swiss. Top each hot burger with a thin slice of blue cheese 1 or 2 minutes before end of broiling time; let cheese soften. Yield: 4 dinner-size servings.

CHEESY-TOMATO BURGERS: Shape meat into 6 or 8 patties. Spoon 1 tablespoon of Cheese Butter (see page 58) on each hot burger before removing from grill. Cover with hot canned French fried or grilled fresh onion rings and favorite barbecue sauce (see page 56). Serve in toasted buns or as meat entrée. Yield: 6 or 8 servings.

COPENHAGEN BURGERS: Combine and mix ¼ cup room temperature cream cheese, ¼ cup crumbled blue cheese, 1 tablespoon finely chopped chives or green onion tops and ½ teaspoon minced parsley. Shape meat into 8 patties. Just before removing from grill spread ½ tablespoon cheese mixture onto 4 patties. Cover with remaining patties. Top each burger with ½ tablespoon cheese mixture and a sprig of watercress or 2 or 3 thin slices of crisp cucumber. Yield: 4 dinner-size servings.

DILLY BURGERS: Add 1 teaspoon dill weed to meat before mixing. Shape into 6 or 8 patties. Brush burgers with Dill Butter (see page 58) several times during broiling. Top each burger with a slice of Mozzarella or American cheese about 2 minutes before end of broiling time; let cheese soften. Top each burger with a bacon curl and a sprig of fresh dill or parsley. Serve in toasted rye, whole wheat or sesame seed buns. Yield: 6 or 8 servings.

FANCY FRENCHY BURGERS: Spread 4 hot dinner-size burgers with French style mustard or Mustard Beer Sauce (see page 56). Top each with 3 thin slices of cucumber and a dollop of salmon caviar. Garnish with a sprig of watercress. Yield: 4 dinner-size servings.

GERMAN HAMBURGERS: Add ¾ teaspoon caraway seed and an additional ¼ cup finely chopped onion to meat before mixing. Top each hamburger with well-drained coleslaw or heated sauerkraut and 1 or 2 thin dill pickle slices. Serve as meat entrée or in toasted rye or sesame seed buns. Yield: 4 dinner-size servings or 8 hamburgers.

ISLAND BURGERS: Prepare ½ recipe Oriental Dipping Sauce (see page 56). Shape meat into 4 dinner-size patties. Brush with sauce several times during broiling. Top each hot burger with 1 or 2 grilled pineapple slices. Garnish with a sprig of watercress; serve with Sweet-Sour Barbecue Sauce (see page 57). Yield: 4 dinner-size servings.

MEXICANA BURGERS: Mash meat of 1 avocado; stir in ½ cup finely chopped fresh tomato or 2 tablespoons chopped sweet red pepper, ¼ cup finely chopped onion, 2 teaspoons lemon juice, ¼ teaspoon salt, ⅛ teaspoon garlic salt and, if desired, 4 to 6 drops hot pepper sauce. Spoon mixture onto 8 hot burgers just before serving. Serve in toasted buns. Yield: About 1¼ cups topping, enough for 8 burgers.

NAPLES BURGERS: Shape meat into 4 or 8 patties. Two minutes before removing from grill top each burger with a slice of provolone cheese; let cheese soften. Top with a thin slice of onion and tomato and a sweet red cherry pepper. Yield: 4 dinner-size servings or 8 burgers.

OLIVE BURGERS: Chop 8 medium-size stuffed olives. Add olives, ¼ teaspoon basil and 1 teaspoon prepared mustard to meat before mixing. Shape into 4 or 8 patties. Before serving top each hot burger with a dollop of catsup and a thin slice of tomato and onion. Garnish with a radish and stuffed olive threaded on a small wooden pick. Serve plain or in toasted whole wheat buns. Yield: 4 dinner-size servings or 8 burgers.

NEW YORK BURGERS: Shape meat into 4 or 8 patties. Brush with Garlic Butter (see page 58) during broiling. Top with fried onion rings and a thin slice of kosher dill pickle or pickled green tomato slice. Serve plain or in toasted buns. Yield: 4 dinner-size servings or 8 burgers.

PEANUT BUTTER BURGERS: Reduce salt to 1¾ teaspoons. Add ½ teaspoon dill weed and ½ cup finely chopped salted peanuts before mixing. Shape into 6 or 8 patties. Top each hot burger with 1 tablespoon peanut butter and 1 or 2 thin dill pickle slices or a crisp bacon curl. Serve plain or in toasted buns. Yield: 6-8 servings.

PEPPER BURGERS: Shape meat into 4 dinner-size patties. A few minutes before end of broiling time top each burger with a slice of American cheese; let cheese soften. Remove from grill and center a large green pepper ring ½ inch thick on cheese. Fill pepper ring with diced fresh tomato and pickled mushrooms or tiny cocktail onions. Yield: 4 dinner-size servings.

PICKLY-CHEESE BURGERS: Combine and mix ½ cup well-drained sweet pickle relish, 2 cups shredded Cheddar cheese, 2 tablespoons chopped onion, 2 tablespoons salad dressing and 1 teaspoon prepared mustard. Shape meat into 8 patties. Two or 3 minutes before end of broiling time spoon an equal amount of cheese mixture onto burgers. Let cheese soften. Serve in toasted rye or sesame seed buns. Yield: 8 servings.

PIZZA BURGERS: Shape meat into 6 or 8 patties. Baste burgers with a commercial Italian dressing while broiling. Two or 3 minutes before end of broiling time top each burger with a thin slice of tomato. Sprinkle with oregano and cover with a slice of Mozzarella cheese. Sprinkle with oregano and top with 2 anchovy fillets. Serve plain or in toasted buns. Yield: 6 or 8 servings.

POCKET BURGERS: Shape meat into 8 patties. Before broiling put two patties together, sandwich-fashion, with a spoonful of relish or small piece of American or Swiss cheese. Seal edges well. Broil. Serve plain or in toasted buns. Yield: 4 servings.

RUSSIAN BURGERS: Shape meat into 8 patties. Spread toasted rye buns with salad dressing. Cover with finely shredded lettuce and a layer of well-drained pickle beet slices. Cover with a hot burger. Spread with prepared mustard. Top with 3 thin hard-cooked egg slices and a dollop of sour cream; cover. Yield: 8 servings.

SOUTHWEST BURGERS: Shape meat into 8 patties. Spread toasted buns with salad dressing. Top each with chopped lettuce, a thin tomato slice, grated sharp Cheddar cheese and a hot burger. Spoon a small amount of hot canned chili con carne with beans over each burger; cover. Yield: 8 servings.

TATER BURGERS: Shape meat into 6 or 8 patties. Just before removing from grill spoon 1 or 2 tablespoons catcup onto each burger. Top with a circle of small hot French fries; sprinkle with chopped green onion or chives. Yield: 6 or 8 servings.

TWO-HIGH BURGERS: Shape meat into 8 patties. When patties are turned the first time, top the cooked side with a thin slice of Bermuda onion and a 3 inch circle of American cheese. Just before serving stack patties 2 high. Center a dollop of catsup and a fried mushroom cap or a few well-drained pickle slices on each. Serve plain or in toasted buns. Yield: 4 dinner-size servings.

Breads To Serve With Burgers

BUNS: Wheat, whole wheat, rye, caraway rye, sesame and black bread buns are all favorites with burgers and are available in most markets.

ROLLS: Hard, poppyseed, Kaiser, Vienna and onion rolls all are delicious with burgers.

BREADS: Slices of French, egg, rye, whole wheat, oatmeal or black bread make bang-up burger sandwiches.

To Toast Buns Or Rolls For Burgers

Split buns and toast to desired brownness, cut side down, on cool portion of grill. Brush with melted butter or margarine or favorite butter spread or sauce (see pages 57 to 59) before adding burger.

LAMB

RACK OF LAMB: A particularly fine cut of lamb. Select a rack of 4 to 9 ribs covered with a thin layer of fat. Excellent for barbecuing on grill in covered cooker or on rotisserie spit.

ROASTS: Leg of lamb (whole or half), bone-in or boned, can be barbecued in covered cooker or on the spit as desired. Lamb shoulder and breast, unless boned and rolled, should be barbecued only in a covered cooker.

Lamb . . . So Tempting, So Tender

Lamb has been a favorite meat for grilling and spit roasting for centuries. Lamb is young tender meat graded Prime, Choice, etc. It is covered with a thin layer of creamy white or slightly pink fat. The lean meat is fine grained, velvety and is light to dark pink in color depending upon age and feed of animal. A parchment-like tissue, or fell, covers the fat, and is usually removed from all cuts except the leg.

Be A Great Lamb Chef

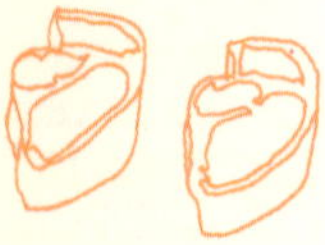

LAMB CHOPS: Select top quality 1 to 2 inch rib, Frenched rib, or center cut loin chops; barbecue on grill or in spit basket.

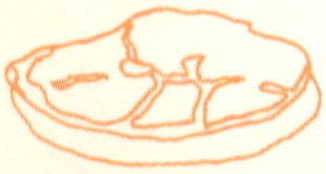

LAMB STEAKS: One to two inch slices cut from shoulder or leg. Barbecue on grill or in spit basket.

Barbecued Lamb Chops

How Much To Buy

CUT	ALLOWANCE PER SERVING
CHOPS and STEAKS	½ to ¾ pound (1 or 2 chops or 1 steak)
ROASTS	
Leg, bone-in	¼ to ½ pound
Leg, boneless	¼ to ⅓ pound
Shoulder, bone-in	½ to ¾ pound
Rack of ribs	½ to ¾ pound (1 or 2 ribs)

Note: See page 14 for information about heat and for ways to gauge temperature at spit or grill level.

How To Barbecue

GRILLED LAMB CHOPS OR STEAKS: Trim excess fat from chops or steaks and marinate, if desired (see marinade recipes page 59). Drain chops or steaks. Arrange ¾ to 1 inch apart on well-greased **MEDIUM** hibachi or grill 3 inches above heat and sear quickly on both sides, turning once. Lower heat source or raise grill; continue barbecuing meat 4 inches from **MEDIUM** heat until tender and the doneness desired, turning once. See Tests For Doneness below. Allow 10 to 15 minutes for a side for 1 inch chops and steaks, 20 minutes a side for 2 inch chops and steaks. Brush meat with oil or favorite basting sauce while barbecuing. Season as desired and serve with favorite sauce (see page 56).

Spit Roasted Lamb Chops and Steaks

Trim excess fat from chops or steaks and marinate, if desired (see marinade recipes page 59). Drain and arrange in lightly greased spit basket. Close basket; attach to rotisserie spit. Barbecue at **LOW** to **MEDIUM** heat (325°F. to 350°F.) at spit level, basting occasionally, until done, with oil, melted butter or basting sauce. Allow 25 to 35 minutes for 1 inch chops or steaks, 40 to 50 minutes for 2 inch ones.

To Test Chops and Steaks For Doneness

Cooked chops and steaks should be crusty brown on the outside, juicy and delicately pink inside. Rare to medium done lamb is preferred by most lamb fanciers. Make a small slash in chop or steak near bone with point of sharp knife. Examine color of meat; it should be juicy and have a faint pink color.

Roast Leg of Lamb

Variations

Grill or spit roast lamb chops or steaks as directed at left and change as suggested below:

BARBECUED LAMB CHOPS OR STEAKS: Baste meat with Barbecue Sauce (see page 56) 3 or 4 times during last 5 or 10 minutes of barbecuing. Serve with remaining sauce.

CURRIED LAMB CHOPS OR STEAKS: Baste meat 3 or 4 times during last 5 or 10 minutes of barbecuing with Curry Butter Or Basting Sauce (see page 58). Serve with Curry or Curried Orange Sauce (see page 56).

MINTED LAMB CHOPS OR STEAKS: Combine 1 jar (8 ounces) mint jelly and ½ cup light corn syrup. Heat slowly until jelly melts; stir in ½ teaspoon mint extract. Baste meat 3 or 4 times during cooking with mint sauce. Serve with remaining sauce.

SWEET 'N SOUR LAMB CHOPS OR STEAKS: Marinate meat in Orange Sherry Marinade (see page 59) before cooking. Baste meat 3 or 4 times during cooking with leftover marinade. Serve with Sweet Sour Sauce or Sweet-Sour Barbecue Sauce (see pages 56 and 57).

LAMB KABOBS: See Kabobs And Skewer Cooking pages 52 to 54).

BARBECUED BREAST OF LAMB: Place a 3 to 4 pound lamb breast over **LOW** heat on greased grill 4 inches from heat. Cook until well browned and meat is fork tender, turning once. Brush with Barbecue or Southwestern Barbecue Sauce (see page 56) 3 or 4 times during cooking. Yield: About 4 servings.

Roast Leg of Lamb

Gourmet INTERNATIONAL™

Plunge 16 jabs (about 1 inch deep) into meaty part of 5 to 7 pound leg of lamb with sharp pointed paring knife. Cut 4 garlic cloves lengthwise into quarters. Push a sliver of garlic into each cut. Rub outside of meat with 1 teaspoon salt. Cook in one of following ways:

TO SPIT ROAST LEG OF LAMB. *See photo at left.* Slide one fork or prong into rotisserie spit, points away from handle. Insert spit into meat almost parallel to bone. Slide second prong onto spit, points towards meat. Push prongs firmly into meat; tighten fork screws with a pliers. Roll spit, back and forth in palms of hands. If spit rolls smoothly meat is well balanced on spit. If unbalanced readjust meat on spit.

Insert meat thermometer, at an angle, with the tip away from spit, bone or fat pocket. Be sure thermometer is inserted so it doesn't touch top, grill or coals when rotating. Attach spit and turn on motor.

Barbecue over **LOW** to **MEDIUM** heat (325°-350°F.) at spit level until browned, tender and meat thermometer reads 140° to 150°F. for rare or medium or 175° to 180°F. for well done lamb. See page 14 for ways to gauge spit level temperature without thermometer and page 14 for adjusting heat when spit roasting. Baste during last 30 minutes of roasting with favorite basting or barbecue sauce (see recipes page 56).

BARBECUED LEG OF LAMB IN COVERED COOKER: Insert thermometer tip into center of thickest part of leg with tip away from bone or fat pocket. Arrange lamb on top grill over drip pan or on a rack in shallow pan on grill. Cover; cook with dampers open or as directed by manufacturers until browned, tender and meat thermometer has reached an internal temperature of 140° to 150°F. for rare or medium or 175° to 180°F. for well done.

Most lamb fanciers feel lamb should be cooked rare to medium, others like it cooked to the well-done stage.

Barbecuing Time For Lamb Roast

Recommended Cooking Temperature . . . 325° to 350°F.; **LOW** to **MEDIUM,** at Spit or Grill Level.

CUT	WEIGHT (Pounds)	APPROX. COOKING TIME (Minutes Per Pound) RARE 140°F.	MEDIUM 150°F.	WELL DONE 175° to 180°F.
LEG				
Bone-in	5-8	14-16	18-20	25-30
Boned, rolled	4-7	15-18	20-22	30-35
SHOULDER				
Bone-in	4-6	14-18	20-22	25-30
Boned, rolled	3-5	15-20	22-25	25-30
RACK OF RIBS	4-5	15-20	22-25	35-40

PORK

Pork and ham, sizzling on the grill, turning on the rotisserie or browning in a covered cooker is always tempting!

Pork has gone modern! Now hams, pork loins, chops and steaks are trimmed free of excess fat leaving only that which is necessary to protect the meat during cooking and make it juicy and deliciously tender.

Research shows the cooking time of fresh pork can be shortened. Now 170°F. is the recommended internal temperature for thoroughly cooked fresh pork cuts, 160°F. for ham that requires cooking before eating and 140°F. for fully-cooked ham.

Be A Wise Buyer of Fresh and Cured Smoked Pork

Fresh pork is seldom graded or branded. Selecting good pork is relatively easy, it has uniform covering or edging of firm white fat and the lean is firm, fine grained, marbled with fat, and has a grayish pink color.

Hams, Canadian bacon and smoked shoulder butts are great cook-out meats. They're available fully cooked, needing only heating and browning, and uncooked, requiring thorough cooking before eating. Cured and smoked meats are usually packaged and labeled. Read labels carefully, they tell whether thorough cooking or just heating to serving temperature is necessary.

What To Buy

PORK LOIN ROASTS: Center cut pork loin (4 to 6 pounds) is excellent for barbecuing on spit or in a covered cooker. Loin ends with the bone in are best barbecued in a covered cooker since bone structure makes it difficult to mount and balance them on a spit.

Backbone should always be sawed from rib, not into meat, for easier carving.

PORK SHOULDER, BONELESS OR ROLLED: Weighs 4 to 6 pounds. Boned, rolled and tied, it's excellent for spit or covered cooker barbecuing.

FRESH HAM (Sometimes called Fresh Pork Leg Roast): Same cut as a bone-in ham except it's fresh pork. Available also boned, rolled and tied. Fine for spit or covered cooker barbecuing.

LOIN CHOPS (Fresh and Smoked): Cut from center of pork loin; have T-shaped bone and a small section of tenderloin attached to bone. Cut 1 to 2 inches thick. Excellent for grilling or barbecuing in spit basket.

RIB CHOPS (Fresh and Smoked): Cut from forward section of pork loin. Cut 1 to 1½ inches thick. Excellent for grilling or barbecuing in spit basket.

SHOULDER CHOPS OR STEAKS: Blade and arm bone pork steaks from shoulder. Cut 1 to 1¼ inches thick. Excellent for barbecuing in hinged broiler or spit basket.

SPARERIBS: See page 33 for complete information.

CANNED HAM: Available in 4 to 14 pound cans. Check label for storage directions. Excellent for spit barbecuing, kabobs, or slicing and grilling. Canned ham is thoroughly cooked, needs only heating and browning.

BONE-IN FULLY-COOKED HAM (Whole or Half): Needs only heating and browning. Fine for barbecuing on spit, in covered cooker or slicing for cooking on grill or in spit basket.

BONE-IN CURED AND SMOKED HAM (Whole or Half): Must be cooked thoroughly before eating! Prepare as suggested for fully-cooked bone-in ham.

BONELESS ROLLED FULLY-COOKED HAM: Slice and grill or barbecue in spit basket. Leave whole or cut in half; tie securely, 1 to 1½ inches apart, the length of the ham and spit roast or barbecue in covered cooker.

SMOKED PORK SHOULDER BUTT (Sometimes called Cottage Butt): Cured and smoked pork. Some are fully-cooked, others need complete cooking. Read label directions. Excellent for spit roasting or slicing and pan frying or barbecuing in hinged broiler.

CANADIAN BACON: Boned, rolled, cured and smoked pork loin, usually fully-cooked. Available in a piece or sliced, thick (¼ inch) or thin (⅛ inch). Whole piece can be spit roasted. Thick slices can be barbecued in hinged broiler, thin slices pan fried.

HAM STEAK: Slice fully-cooked bone-in or boneless ham ¾ to 2 inches thick. Barbecue in well-greased hinged broiler on grill or in spit basket.

How Much to Buy

MEAT	APPROXIMATE SERVINGS PER POUND (Raw Weight)
BONE-IN FRESH LOIN, ham, chops, steaks, cook-before-eating ham	2 to 3
BONELESS loins, fresh ham	3
BONELESS FULLY COOKED HAM, canned ham, Canadian bacon, smoked butts	3 to 4

How To Barbecue

Fresh and smoked pork cuts barbecue perfectly on the hibachi, grill, in covered cookers or on the rotisserie. Here are the favorite ways of cooking these popular meats:

Grilled Pork Chops, Fresh or Smoked

Arrange fresh or smoked rib, loin or shoulder chops on well-greased hibachi or grill or in hinged broiler. Place on grill 4 to 6 inches from **LOW** to **MEDIUM** heat. Brown chops on first side (see Approximate Cooking Time below). Turn chops; barbecue until well browned, thoroughly cooked and fork tender. Brush chops frequently during cooking with oil, melted butter or margarine or favorite basting sauce (see page 56). Serve plain or with favorite sauce.

Barbecuing Time For Pork

Recommended Heat—**LOW** to **MEDIUM** (325 to 350°F.).

THICKNESS OF CHOP (Inches)	APPROXIMATE COOK TIME * (Minutes) FIRST SIDE	SECOND SIDE
1	15 to 18	15 to 18
1½	20 to 25	18 to 20
2	28 to 30	25 to 30

*Must be thoroughly cooked (170°F. internal temperature).

Broiled Ham Slices

Arrange ½ to 1 inch slices of canned or boneless fully-cooked ham in well-greased hinged broiler or directly on **MEDIUM** hibachi or grill about 4 inches from heat. Brush with favorite basting or barbecue sauce (see page 56). Turn when slices are lightly browned on first side; brush with sauce and brown second side, 4 to 5 minutes a side.

Spit Barbecuing Pork

Pork loins, fresh ham, smoked or canned hams, Canadian bacon, smoked pork shoulder butts, etc.

The size and weight of meat being barbecued on the rotisserie spit is limited by the length and sturdiness of the spit and the power of the motor. Read and follow directions for spit roasting supplied by the manufacturer of the equipment being used or the following general directions:

Trim off any excess fat. Tie boneless roasts securely with heavy string (butcher's cord, if possible) 1½ inches apart the length of the roast. Slip one prong or fork onto spit, points away from handle. Push spit lengthwise through center of meat so it is balanced on spit. Slide second prong or fork onto spit; push prongs into meat.

Test spit for balance. Roll spit back and forth on palm of hands. If it turns smoothly it is well balanced. Readjust spit in meat if necessary.

Tighten prong screws with a pliers. Insert meat thermometer at a slight angle with tip in the center of thickest part of meat away from spit, bone or fat pocket. Attach spit to motor of preheated unit. Make sure thermometer clears hood or cover, grill and briquets when rotating. Spit level temperature should be **MEDIUM** (350-375°F.). See pages 14 and 15 to judge temperature and for information on drip pan.

Barbecue meat until fork tender and it has reached a proper internal temperature (170°F. for fresh pork, 160°F. for cook-before-eating smoked pork and 140°F. for fully-cooked smoked pork or canned hams).

Brush 3 or 4 times during last 30 minutes barbecuing with favorite barbecue sauce (see pages 56 and 57) if desired. Cool 15 to 20 minutes before carving.

Variations

Follow recipe for pork or ham barbecued on spit or in covered cooker; change as follows:

POLYNESIAN-STYLE PORK OR HAM: Prepare the following sauce. Combine 1 jar (10 ounces) orange marmalade, ¼ cup each of catsup and pineapple juice, 2 tablespoons lemon juice or vinegar and ½ teaspoon allspice; heat, stirring constantly. Simmer gently 2 or 3 minutes. Baste roast with glaze 3 or 4 times during last 30 minutes of roasting. Serve remaining sauce with meat. Garnish with fresh or canned pineapple, banana chunks rolled in lime juice, honey and toasted coconut and mint sprigs. Yield: 8 to 12 servings.

PORK LOIN OR HAM À LA ORANGE: Combine ½ cup orange marmalade with ¼ cup orange juice for glaze. Baste roast with glaze 3 or 4 times during last 30 minutes of barbecuing. Sprinkle roast before serving with fine shreds of orange rind. Garnish with orange twists and watercress. Serve plain or with Orange Sauce With Cointreau (see page 56). Yield: 8 to 12 servings.

SWEET SOUR PORK LOIN: Baste with Sweet-Sour Barbecue Sauce (see page 56) 3 or 4 times during last 25 minutes of roasting. Serve with remaining sauce. Yield: 8 to 12 servings.

PEANUTTY PORK ROAST: Baste roast with a mixture of ¼ cup smooth peanut butter and ⅓ cup apricot preserves 3 or 4 times during last 25 minutes of roasting. Sprinkle roast with finely chopped peanuts before serving. Serve with Curried Orange Sauce (see page 56). Yield: 8 to 12 servings.

Barbecuing Time For Pork Roast

MEAT AND CUT	APPROX. WEIGHT (Pounds)	COOK TO INTERNAL TEMP. (Degrees F.)	COOK—MINUTES PER POUND*
PORK, FRESH			
LOIN			
Center	4-6	170	30-35
Half	5-7	170	35-40
Boneless, rolled	4-6	170	35-40
LEG			
Whole, bone-in	12-14	170	22-26
Whole, boneless, rolled	10-12	170	24-28
FULLY-COOKED HAMS			
Whole, bone-in	10-14	140	15-18
Half, bone-in	5-7	140	18-24
Boneless, rolled	8-10	140	15-18
COOK-BEFORE-EATING HAM			
Whole, bone-in	10-14	160	18-20
Half, bone-in	5-7	160	22-25
CANADIAN BACON	4-6	160	24-26
SMOKED SHOULDER BUTT			
Fully-Cooked	3-4	140	30-35
Cook-Before-Eating	3-4	160	35-40

*Recommended cooking temperature 325 to 350°F. at spit or grill level.

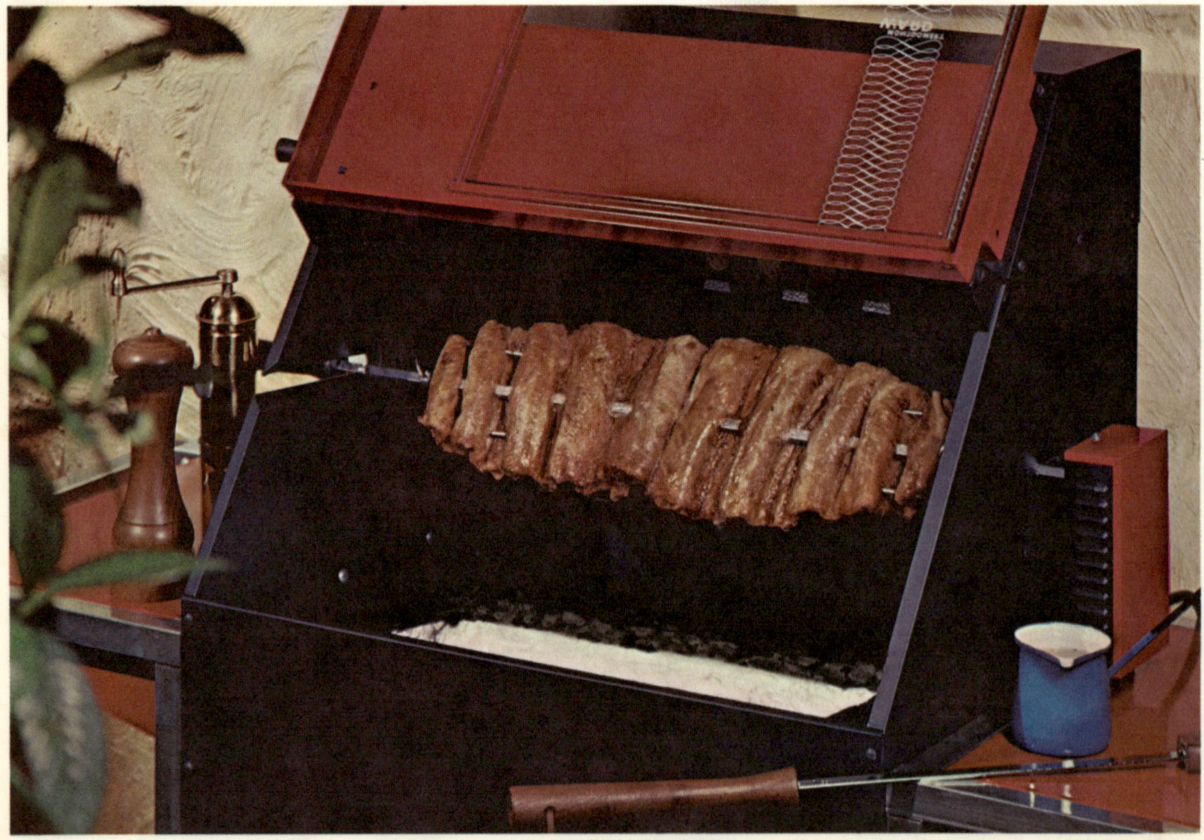

Spareribs Laced on Spit

Spareribs

WHAT TO BUY: Slabs of spareribs, back or barbecue ribs.

HOW MUCH TO BUY: Allow 1 to 1¼ pounds of uncooked ribs per person.

SEASONING: Sprinkle salt evenly over ribs allowing about ¼ teaspoon of salt per pound of ribs. Marinate, If desired, 2 to 12 hours before barbecuing. See recipes for marinades on page 59.

BASTE: During barbecuing with leftover marinade or favorite basting sauce. Baste during last 15 to 20 minutes with favorite barbecue or sweet sour sauce. See recipes on page 56.

HOW TO COOK: See 4 Ways To Cook Spareribs, Back or Barbecue Ribs below.

TO LACE RIBS ON ROTISSERIE SPIT: Slip one prong or fork onto spit, points away from handle. Beginning with narrow end of ribs run spit through center, accordion fashion (Fig. 1). Start next slab of ribs at wide end and repeat process (Fig. 2). Center ribs on spit. Slip second prong onto spit points towards meat. Push prongs into meat firmly! Balance and tighten screws with pliers. Run several metal skewers through meat, parallel to spit to keep ribs from slipping.

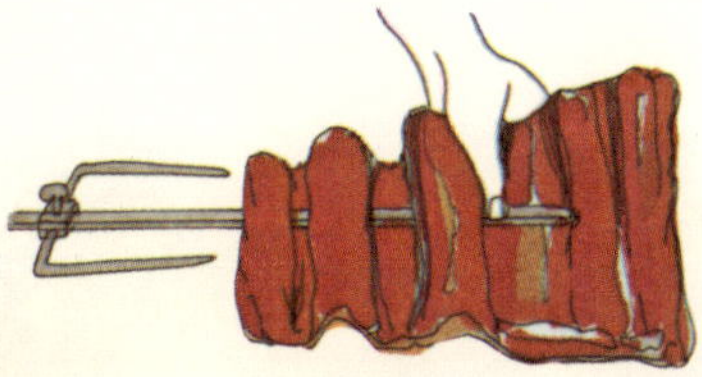

Figure 1

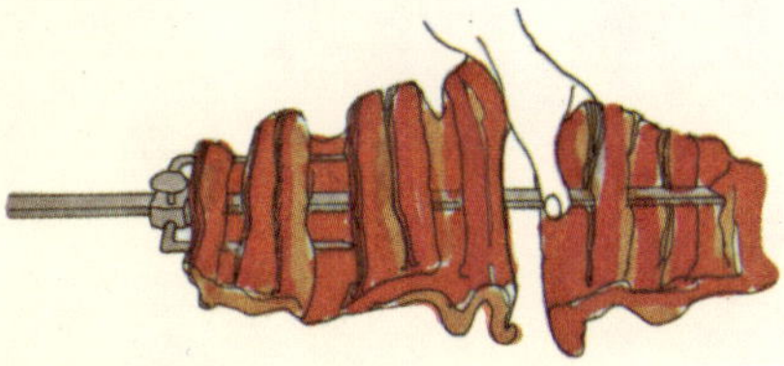

Figure 2

4 Ways To Cook Spareribs, Back or Barbecue Ribs

See pages 56 to 59 for sauces, marinades and basting sauces.

ON THE HIBACHI OR GRILL: Salt ribs (¼ teaspoon per pound), arrange bone side down on grill, 5 to 7 inches from **LOW** heat. Barbecue 20 to 25 minutes. Turn ribs; brown meat side of ribs 8 to 10 minutes. Turn meat, bone side down and barbecue 20 to 25 minutes. Brush meat side of ribs with favorite sauce; barbecue without turning until meat is tender, 20 to 25 minutes, basting occasionally. During last few minutes brush both top and underside of ribs with sauce.

IN COVERED COOKER: Arrange seasoned slabs of ribs on grill or in rib rack in covered cooker over drip pan. Roast over **MEDIUM** heat with dampers open, or as manufacturer of equipment directs, until ribs are browned and meat is tender, 1½ to 2 hours. Baste with favorite sauce (see page 56) during last few minutes of barbecuing.

LACED ON ROTISSERIE SPIT. *See photo at left.* Marinate spareribs, if desired. Lace ribs on rotisserie spit as directed on this page. Attach spit and start motor. Roast at **MEDIUM** heat (350°F.) at spit level until ribs are nicely browned and tender, 1½ to 2 hours. See page 14 for estimating spit level temperature. Baste with leftover marinade or basting sauce during last few minutes of barbecuing.

IN SPIT BASKET: Cut spareribs into 2 to 4 rib portions. Sprinkle evenly with salt. Place in spit basket, lock cover in place. Put basket onto spit. Attach spit, start motor. Barbecue over **MEDIUM** heat (350°F.) at spit level until ribs are nicely browned and meat is tender and pulls away from the bones about 1½ hours. See page 14 for method of estimating temperature at spit level. Baste with favorite basting sauce during barbecuing, if desired. Brush last 10 minutes of barbecuing with favorite barbecue sauce; serve with additional sauce.

Variations

Barbecue ribs in one of the 4 Ways To Cook Spareribs suggested above; change as follows:

SOUTHWESTERN BARBECUED RIBS: Baste ribs while barbecuing with Bar-B-Q Basting Sauce (see page 58). Brush during last 15 to 20 minutes of barbecuing with Barbecue or Southwestern Barbecue Sauce (see page 56). Serve with additional sauce.

POLYNESIAN RIBS: Cut ribs into 3 or 4 rib portions; marinate 2 to 4 hours in Sherry Soy Marinade (see page 59). Drain ribs and barbecue in spit basket. Baste during roasting with leftover marinade. Serve with Sweet-Sour Barbecue or Curried Orange Sauce (see page 56). Garnish platter, if desired, with orange and pineapple slices, strawberries and watercress or mint sprigs.

LUAU RIBS: Marinate ribs in Oriental Marinade (see page 59), if desired. Lace seasoned spareribs on rotisserie spit. See directions on this page. Brush with Oriental Dipping or Sweet Sour Sauce (pages 56 and 57) during last 15 to 20 minutes of roasting. Garnish platter with fresh or canned pineapple slices, melon wedges and clusters of green or red grapes, if desired.

SWEET SOUR RIBS: Marinate spareribs 2 to 4 hours in Pineapple Wine Marinade (see page 59). Drain ribs; lace on rotisserie spit, see directions on this page. Barbecue, basting often with leftover marinade. Serve with Sweet Sour Sauce or Sweet-Sour Barbecue Sauce (see pages 56 and 57).

SAUSAGE

Sausage and Canned Meats . . . Cook-Out Favorites

Sausages and canned meats are great penny pinching foods and ideal ones for cook-outs. They're convenient to tote to cook-out site, quick to fix and can be turned into scores of tempting dishes.

Sausage

There's a sausage to please most every taste. Many of the favorites are now available fully-cooked and need only a quick heating and browning. Read the package labels carefully! All sausages not labeled fully-cooked or ready-to-eat must be precooked before grilling or cooked very slowly until thoroughly done.

So, try to select fully-cooked sausages for grill cooking; they heat in a hurry and watchers are always eager eaters.

These are some of the favorite cook-out sausages:

FRANKS, WIENERS, SMOKY LINKS, RING BOLOGNA AND KNOCKWURST: Are made of finely ground beef, pork and veal. Most brands are fully-cooked and can be heated and ready to serve in minutes.

BRATWURST: Fully-cooked bratwurst is now available in most markets, ready for quick heating and browning. Uncooked (raw) sausages must be given a long slow barbecuing or be precooked. To precook bratwurst arrange links in frying pan, cover with cold water, heat to simmering stage and let stand in water 10 minutes. Drain and barbecue as directed for fully-cooked links.

PORK SAUSAGE LINKS: Brown 'n serve ones are ideal for grill barbecuing. They are fully-cooked and can be heated quickly. Uncooked links require long slow barbecuing until thoroughly done.

A Grilled Sausage Wheels Page 35
B Sausage Links Page 35
C Pork Sausage Links
D Ring Bologna Page 34
E Franks
F Knockwurst
G Bratwurst

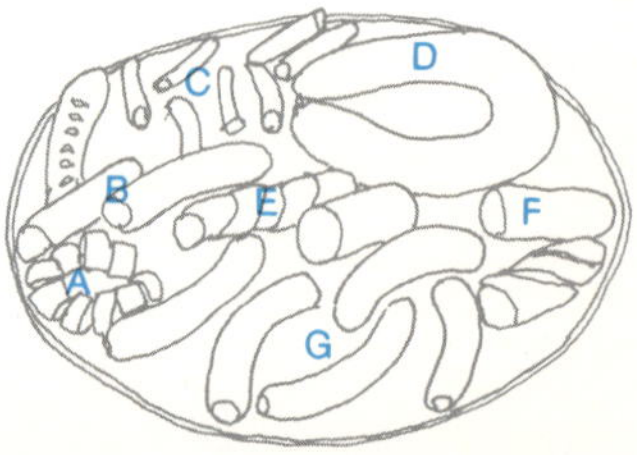

Canned Meats

Most canned meats are fully-cooked and can be stored on the shelf and prepared on the patio grill or carried miles away to be turned into wonderful dinners with little effort. The more popular canned meats such as beef stew, corned beef hash, Vienna sausages, luncheon meat and chopped ham require no refrigeration before opening.

Most canned hams require refrigeration prior to use. Check the label carefully; it will tell whether the ham should be refrigerated.

4 Ways To Grill Sausage Links

SAUSAGE LINKS COOKED IN HINGED BROILER: Arrange favorite assortment of fully-cooked sausage links (franks, wieners, bratwurst, smoky links, knockwurst, pork sausage links, etc.) in well-greased hinged broiler; close. Place on **MEDIUM** hibachi or grill, 4 to 6 inches from heat. Brown and bring to serving temperature, turning hinged broiler once during heating. Serve plain or in buttered toasted buns with favorite fixings.

SAUSAGE LINKS COOKED ON GRILL: Arrange fully-cooked sausage links on **LOW** to **MEDIUM** hibachi or grill 4 to 6 inches above heat. Brown and heat links turning once with tongs.

GRILLED BUTTERFLY SAUSAGE LINKS: Follow recipe for Sausage Links except split sausage links lengthwise, not quite through, before arranging in well-greased hinged broiler, hibachi or grill.

FRANK OR SAUSAGE SANDWICH, PIZZA STYLE: Split 8 long (5 or 6 inch) hard rolls in half; spread cut surfaces with Garlic or Onion Butter (see page 58). Combine and mix 2 cups shredded Mozzarella cheese, ½ cup shredded Parmesan cheese and 2 teaspoons oregano. Sprinkle an equal amount of cheese mixture over bottom of each roll; cover with top. Wrap securely in a double thick 10 inch square of heavy duty foil. Place to one side of **MEDIUM** hibachi or grill 4 to 6 inches from heat while franks, wieners, smoked sausage links or knockwurst heat and brown (see page 34). To serve unwrap roll; open carefully. Place hot Grilled Butterfly Sausage Link (this page) on cheese. Add catsup or chili sauce as desired; close. Yield: 8 sandwiches.

GRILLED SAUSAGE WHEELS: Select fully-cooked franks, wieners, smoky links or knockwurst. Make slashes the length of the sausage ½ inch apart, not quite through (see photo page 34). Skewer ends of each sausage together with a short metal skewer or wooden pick. Arrange on **LOW** to **MEDIUM** grill, 4 to 5 inches from heat. Brown and bring to serving temperature; turn once. Brush with Barbecue Sauce (see page 56 and 57) during last few minutes of grilling, if desired.

More Sausage Treats

CRISPY HOT DOG SANDWICH: Prepare Grilled Butterfly Sausage Links (this page) using franks or wieners. Spread toasted hot dog buns with Herb or Mustard Butter (see page 58). Cover bottom bun halves with well-drained coleslaw. Top each with crisp pickle slices and a butterfly frank. Drizzle mustard or catsup over frank.

GIANT HOT DOG SANDWICH: Prepare Grilled Sausage Wheels (this page) using franks or wieners. Cover bottom half of each buttered toasted hamburger bun with a lettuce leaf, Cheddar cheese slice, thin Bermuda onion and tomato slice and a ring of green pepper. Top with a sausage wheel. Drizzle with catsup, chili sauce or hot dog pickle relish and cover with bun top.

ALOHA-SAUSAGE SANDWICHES: Prepare Grilled Sausage Wheels (this page) using franks or smoky links. Spread cut surfaces of toasted hamburger buns with Orange Marmalade Or Apricot Butter (see page 58). Cover bottom half of each bun with a grilled canned pineapple slice; top with a sausage wheel and drizzle with Pineapple Barbecue Sauce (see page 56). Cover with bun top.

MEXICANA FRANKS: Prepare Grilled Butterfly Sausage Links (this page) using franks or wieners. Spread cut surfaces of toasted hot dog buns with Mustard Butter (see page 58). Top bottom half of each bun with a butterfly frank. Spoon hot chili con carne with beans over frank. Top with shredded Cheddar cheese and thin hot chili peppers, if desired. Cover with bun top.

HOAKI HOT DOGS: Prepare Grilled Sausage Wheels (this page) using franks. Cover bottom of each buttered toasted hamburger bun with a leaf of lettuce, two thin slices of Swiss cheese, a slice of tomato and Bermuda onion. Cover with sausage wheel and hot dog pickle relish or catsup. Cover with bun top.

BERLINER FRANKS: Cover bottom of each buttered toasted hot dog bun with thin slice of brick cheese; cover with drained hot sauerkraut and slice of kosher dill pickle. Top with hot grilled frank and spread with mustard. Cover with bun top.

SMOKY FRANKS: Prepare Grilled Butterfly Sausage Links (this page) using franks or wieners. Spread buttered toasted bottom half of hot dog buns with a smoky cheese spread; sprinkle with crisp bacon bits and top with a butterfly frank. Drizzle with catsup or mustard. Cover with bun top.

FRANKS, AMERICAN-STYLE: Combine and mix 1 jar (8 ounces) triple-use cheese spread and 1½ teaspoons prepared mustard. Center a hot grilled frank (see page 34) on buttered grilled hot dog bun. Top with cheese mixture, well-drained sweet pickle relish and finely chopped onion. Serve with catsup and mustard. Yield: About 1 cup sauce, enough for 6 to 8 frank sandwiches.

FISH AND SEAFOOD

A Few Facts About Fish Cookery

Use only quality fresh fish; clean and refrigerate at once.

Select a lean fish for grilling, it will hold its shape during barbecuing. Baste fish frequently during barbecuing to keep fish moist.

When a fatty fish is used, basting is not usually required.

Fish is delicate and fragile. Handle carefully and as little as possible before cooking. Be sure to oil grill or basket well as the skin of fish is delicate and will stick to the grill when you turn or remove fish.

Wash, drain and dry fish with paper toweling.

Use a long handled well-greased hinged broiler for cooking fish, it will be easier to turn and will retain its shape, or use a spit basket.

Don't overcook fish. It is done when meat flakes easily when tested with fork.

How Much To Buy or Catch

For each adult serving allow: ⅓ to ½ pound boneless fish or seafood; or, 1 pound whole fish.

Rainbow Trout or Other Small Fish

See photo at left

Scale fresh fish; clean, wash and dry. Arrange in well-greased long handled hinged broiler. Place on **MEDIUM** hibachi or grill 4 to 6 inches above heat. Barbecue 7 to 10 minutes, basting often with melted butter or margarine, Herb Butter Or Basting Sauce (see page 58). Turn; cook until fish will flake easily when tested with a fork, about 8 to 10 minutes. Serve with salt, pepper and melted butter, Herb Butter or Barbecue Sauce. Yield: Allow an 8 to 12 ounce fish per person.

Crusty Crumb Coated Rainbow Trout . . . or Other Small Fish

Clean, wash and dry pan-dressed fish. Dip each fish in an egg-milk mixture (allow 1 large egg, beaten, ¼ cup milk and 1 teaspoon salt for 6 half pound fish); roll in dry cereal, bread or cracker crumbs or half and half, flour and corn meal. Fry fish in single layer in hot bacon drippings or other fat in heavy frying pan on **MEDIUM** hibachi or grill 4 to 6 inches from heat until brown. Turn carefully; brown second side and cook until done. Cooked fish will flake easily when tested with fork. Serve with Dill or Lemony Butter Or Basting Sauce (see page 58). Yield: 6 servings.

Types of Fish for Outdoor Barbecuing

WHOLE FISH: Must be scaled, drawn, washed and dried before cooking. If desired, the head, tail and fins can be removed. Examples: Lake trout, white fish, striped bass, rainbow trout, etc.

DRESSED OR PAN-DRESSED FISH: Ready to cook. Fish has been scaled, drawn, and has head, fins and tail removed. Examples: Rainbow trout, ocean perch, yellow perch, catfish, etc.

STEAKS: Ready to cook. Cross section slices cut from large fish. Slices 1 to 1½ inches thick are best for grilling. Examples: Salmon, halibut, snapper, swordfish, sablefish, king mackerel, etc.

FILLETS: Are the whole sides of the fish cut along the backbone from head to tail. Some require scaling and skinning, others are skinned or scaled with skin left on. Scale and skin, if required; wash and dry. Examples: Lake trout, whitefish, salmon, pike, mackerel, yellow perch, snapper, flounder, etc.

FISH PORTIONS OR STICKS: Ready to cook. They are breaded boneless squares or sticks of fish, sometimes precooked.

Spit Barbecued Rainbow Trout or Other Small Fish

Arrange cleaned fish (rainbow or brook trout, catfish, flounder, small mackerel or other small fish) in single layer in well oiled spit basket. Adjust cover so it holds fish in place without tearing skin. Attach basket to spit. Attach spit and start motor. Cook over **MEDIUM** heat 12 to 18 minutes depending upon size of fish. Baste occasionally with Herb, Lemony or Dill Butter (see page 58). Fish is done when flesh flakes easily when tested with fork. Serve with salt, pepper and Barbecue Sauce (see page 56) or the remaining flavored butter used for basting. Yield: Allow 1 to 1¼ pound fish per serving.

Fish Steaks and Fillets

Marinate fish, (See recipes for marinades on page 59.) if desired; drain. Arrange 1 to 1½ inch steaks, whole or serving size portions of fillets on long handled well-greased hinged broilers. Place on **MEDIUM** hibachi or grill 4 to 6 inches from heat. Barbecue 6 to 7 minutes; turn and cook until fish flakes easily when tested with fork. Baste often during broiling with favorite butter or basting sauce (see pages 57 to 59) or leftover marinade. Serve with melted butter or margarine or Barbecue Sauce (see page 56).

◀ Rainbow Trout

Broiled Fish Portions or Sticks

Dip frozen raw breaded fish portions or sticks in oil or melted Curry, Herb or Lemony Butter (see page 58). Place in single layer in long handled well-greased hinged broiler. Place on **MEDIUM** hibachi or grill 4 to 6 inches from heat and cook 6 to 8 minutes; turn and cook until fish flakes easily when tested with a fork. Serve with Barbecue, Cucumber or Coral Sauce (see pages 56 and 57).

Spit Barbecued Whole Fish

Select a 4 to 6 pound dressed fresh or defrosted frozen salmon, sablefish, red snapper, whitefish, lake trout, pike, cod or other whole fish; wash carefully and pat cavity and skin dry with paper toweling. Brush cavity with lemon juice and sprinkle with salt and pepper.

Close cavity with small skewers laced with heavy oiled string. Insert rotisserie spit the length of the fish next to the backbone. Balance fish on spit so it will turn smoothly and press forks or prongs into fish; tighten screws. Brush well with oil or melted butter or margarine. If fish is very large it may be necessary to tie it at 1 inch intervals with heavy oiled string. Fish may be placed in a rotisserie basket or wrapped in a chicken wire shield lined, if desired, with washed ferns.

Attach spit to rotisserie motor. Start motor and cook fish 50 to 60 minutes or until it flakes easily when tested with a fork. Serve with Coral, Cucumber or Barbecue Sauce (see pages 56 and 57). Yield: Count on ½ pound of raw fish per person.

Barbecued Stuffed Fish

Wash, dry and stuff a 4 to 6 pound dressed fish with favorite fish stuffing. Close cavity with small skewers laced with oiled string. Brush skin well with oil or favorite flavored butter (see page 57). Place in special long handled fish shaped basket*. Place on **MEDIUM** hibachi or grill 4 to 6 inches from heat source and cook until fish is done, 45 to 60 minutes or until fish flakes easily when tested with a fork. Turn 3 or 4 times during cooking. Baste frequently with melted butter or margarine or favorite flavored butter. Yield: 6 to 8 servings.

*If a fish shaped basket is not available, wrap fish loosely but securely in a triple thickness of heavy duty foil with double fold on top and at ends. Place on **MEDIUM** hibachi or grill 5 to 7 inches from heat, or place on a well-greased double thick foil boat and cook, without turning, in covered cooker.

Barbecued Lobsters

Gourmet INTERNATIONAL™

See photo at right

Select live spiny, rock or northern lobsters (about 1 pound each). Kill lobster instantly by laying it on its back and inserting tip of sharp knife between tail segment and body shell, severing the spinal cord, or insert point of knife in center of small cross at back of head.

Place lobsters over **MEDIUM** hibachi or grill 5 to 7 inches from heat; cook 18 to 20 minutes, turning often, to cook evenly. To serve split lobster in half lengthwise and remove stomach (small sac) behind head. Pull out intestinal vein running down the center and crack the claws. Serve with melted butter and lemon wedges or Lemony Butter (see page 58). Yield: Allow 1 lobster per person.

Barbecued Lobster Tails I

Gourmet INTERNATIONAL™

Remove swimmerettes and sharp edges from 6 (8 ounce) fresh or defrosted frozen spiny or rock lobster tails. Cut off thin undershell membrane and any boney material with kitchen scissors. Wash and dry. Bend tail backwards to crack shell. Place lobster tails, shell side up, on long handled oiled, hinged broiler. Brush meat side with softened Lemony Butter (see page 58). Close and lock hinged broiler. Place on **MEDIUM** hibachi or grill, shell sides up, 5 to 7 inches from heat and broil 3 to 5 minutes or until meat is nicely browned. Turn. Brush meat with Lemony Butter and cook until meat is firm and opaque, 12 to 15 minutes. Baste frequently while barbecuing and serve with Lemony Butter or melted butter, salt, pepper and lemon wedges. Yield: Allow one 8 ounce lobster tail per person.

Barbecued Lobster Tails II

Gourmet INTERNATIONAL™

See photo at right

Clean 6 (8 ounce) fresh or defrosted frozen spiny or rock lobster tails as directed above. Bend tail backwards to crack shell, this prevents lobster tail from curling. Proceed as directed for Barbecued Lobster Tails I above except barbecue tails directly on hibachi or grill rather than in hinged broiler. Yield: Allow one 8 ounce lobster tail per person.

Clambake

Cut 6 double thick sheets of heavy duty foil 18 x 36 inches. Top each with a double thick piece of cheesecloth the same size. Wash shells of 6 dozen steamer clams. Peel 12 small onions. Wash 6 baking potatoes. Remove husks and silk from 6 ears of corn.

Center a live 1 pound lobster (about) or 2 live blue crabs on cheese cloth. Surround with 2 onions, a potato, an ear of corn and 12 clams. Tie opposite ends of cheesecloth together. Fold foil up and around foods. Add 1 cup water and close package securely with a double fold on top and at ends. Repeat until all six packages are prepared.

Arrange packages on **MEDIUM** to **MEDIUM-HIGH** grill with hood, 5 to 7 inches from heat. If grill does not have a hood cover whole grill with heavy duty foil but leave air space around edges. Cook until onions and potatoes are tender, 50 to 60 minutes. To serve, open package; if lobster was used, crack claws. Serve with melted butter and lemon wedges. Yield: 6 servings.

Barbecued Lobster and Lobster Tails II

Barbecued Shrimp

Combine and mix 3 pounds large shrimp, peeled and deveined, and Wine Marinade (see page 59) in a bowl. Cover and refrigerate 2 to 4 hours, stirring several times. Thread shrimp on long skewers. To cook hold over **MEDIUM** to **MEDIUM-HIGH** hibachi or grill, 4 to 6 inches from heat until shrimp are pink and cooked. Brush with marinade during cooking. Remove from skewers and serve with Oriental Dipping Sauce or Barbecue Sauce (see page 56). Yield: About 3 to 4 servings.

Charcoal Broiled Scallops

Wash 2 pounds fresh or defrosted frozen scallops; place in bowl. Add ¾ cup commercial oil and vinegar or Italian dressing. Mix, cover and refrigerate 1 hour. Cut a half bacon slice for each scallop; cook bacon over low heat until about ½ done or until edges start to crinkle; drain. Drain and dry scallops; wrap each scallop in a half slice of bacon. Fasten with wooden pick or small bamboo skewer. Place in long handled hinged broiler. Barbecue on **MEDIUM** hibachi or grill 4 to 6 inches from heat 4 to 5 minutes. Baste frequently with slightly melted Herb, Lemony or Cheese-Chive Butter or Basting Sauce (see page 58). Turn broiler and cook until scallops are cooked and bacon is crisp and brown, 4 to 6 minutes. Serve plain or with remaining flavored butter. Yield: About 6 servings.

Grilled Soft-Shell Crabs

Clean, wash and dry 1 dozen fresh or defrosted frozen soft-shell crabs. Arrange in long handled well-greased hinged broiler. Brush with Lemony Butter or Basting Sauce (see page 58) or melted butter. Place on **MEDIUM** hibachi or grill, 4 to 6 inches from heat 7 or 8 minutes. Turn and barbecue until done and lightly browned, 7 to 8 minutes. Brush often with basting sauce or melted butter. Serve with melted Lemony Butter or lemon wedges. Yield: About 6 servings.

Roasted Oysters

Scrub 24 oysters in shell very well. Arrange on **MEDIUM** to **MEDIUM-HIGH** hibachi or grill 4 to 6 inches above heat; barbecue until shells open. Serve hot with Seafood Sauce or melted butter. Yield: About 4 servings.

Seafood Sauce

Combine and mix ¾ cup catsup or chili sauce, ⅓ cup lemon juice, ¼ cup finely chopped celery, 1½ tablespoons horseradish, ¼ teaspoon salt, ½ teaspoon grated onion, if desired, and 2 drops hot pepper sauce. Yield: About 1¼ cups.

POULTRY

To Prepare Poultry for Spit Barbecuing

Important! Read directions for spit or rotisserie barbecuing supplied by the manufacturer of equipment. The size and strength of spit and rotisserie may limit the size and weight of the bird which can be barbecued.

Remove neck from fresh or fully defrosted bird. Clean, rinse and pat cavities and skin dry with paper toweling.

Season cavities with salt and prepare bird for spit as recipe (see pages 41 and 42) suggests.

Fasten neck skin to back of bird with small metal skewer as size of bird requires, small ones (3 to 3½ inch) for rock Cornish hens, chickens, ducklings and capons and heavier 5 to 6 inch skewers for turkeys.

Close lower body cavity of bird, if stuffed, by sticking small metal skewers across cavity opening and lacing shut with string.

Flatten wings against breast; tie wings to breast securely with string or light weight cord to hold in place during barbecuing.

Press drumsticks under band of skin or tie securely to tail.

Thread one spit prong or fork onto spit, points away from handle. Push spit lengthwise through center of bird starting at neck end. (Any variation of this method will be given in specific recipe, see pages 41 and 42). Slide second spit prong or fork onto spit, points towards bird. Push prongs into poultry.

Check to see if poultry is well balanced on spit. Roll spit back and forth on palms of hands. If spit turns smoothly it is well balanced. Readjust poultry on spit, if necessary, to balance. Tighten prong screws. Note: Food must be balanced on spit to prevent strain on rotisserie motor.

Brush poultry with cooking oil or rub skin with butter.

Insert meat thermometer tip in thick part of thigh or if bird is stuffed insert tip into center of stuffing.

Attach spit to rotisserie; start motor.

After poultry has started to barbecue tiny pin-point bubbles appear on the surface. This assures you that the heat is correct.

A Few Facts About the Heat

Read and follow directions supplied by manufacturer for lighting or building a fire and controlling heat. Here are a few general rules, if no directions are available:

You may need a drip pan. Drip pans are needed in charcoal units but most gas barbecue manufacturers do not suggest the use of one since the ceramic or pumice rocks or briquets are self cleaning.

When a drip pan is needed it should be sturdy metal or heavy foil 1-inch larger all around than the bird being barbecued. See page 11 for directions for making foil drip pans. The drip pan should be placed on a flat surface, never on briquets, parallel to and just in front of center of bird.

Arrange greyed hot charcoal or heated ceramic briquets in fire box or bowl as manufacturer of equipment directs. Charcoal briquets are usually placed behind or around the drip pan. Lower or raise fire box, separate or add coals or turn heat up or down as needed to maintain proper temperature at spit level. See specific recipe (page 14) for recommended spit level temperature.

To Gauge Temperature At Spit Level

Thermometers are available which can be attached to the spit to indicate temperature at spit level. When no thermometer is available hold hand, cautiously, palm side down, under roast and count seconds this way, 1000-1, 1000-2 is **HIGH,** 1000-3 is **MEDIUM-HIGH,** 1000-4 is **MEDIUM** and 1000-5 is **LOW.**

To Check Poultry for Doneness

Whole chickens, capons, rock Cornish hens, ducklings and turkeys are fully cooked when drumsticks can be moved up and down and twisted out of joint easily. Meat on the thickest part of drumstick and breast should be fork tender and feel soft when pressed with finger. Protect fingers with paper toweling or clean cloth.

Chicken, duckling, capon or turkey pieces, quarters and halves are done when meat on drumstick and breast is fork tender. Make a small cut in thickest part of meat near bone with a sharp pointed knife. Examine color of meat. It is done when meat shows no pink color.

Spit Barbecued Chicken

See photo on front cover

3 to 4 pound ready-to-cook broiler fryer chicken
1 teaspoon salt
Stuffing (see recipes page 45), optional
Oil, melted butter or margarine

Prepare chicken and place on spit as directed for spit barbecued poultry on this page. Attach spit to motor above drip pan, or as manufacturer of equipment directs. Brush with oil, melted butter or margarine. Start motor. Barbecue over **MEDIUM** to **MEDIUM-HIGH** heat (about 375°F.) at spit level or as manufacturer of equipment suggests. See fire building and temperature information on page 7 and 14. Barbecue chicken about 1½ to 2 hours, if stuffed, 20 to 25 minutes less if unstuffed. Check chicken for doneness (see methods suggested above). Baste with favorite basting or barbecue sauce (see page 56) during last 20 minutes of barbecuing. Yield: 4 servings.

Spit Barbecued Chickens, Tandem-Style

Roast 2 or 3 (2½ to 4 pound) or the number of ready-to-cook broiler fryer chickens the length the rotisserie spit will allow. Follow recipe for Spit Barbecued Chicken (at left) making sure each chicken is held firmly in place by sticking fork prongs into one end of each chicken being barbecued and two into the last chicken on the spit. Tighten screws. Tie as needed to hold chickens firmly in place. Cook time may have to be lengthened slightly; check leg and breast for doneness (see check for doneness at left) at end of 2 hours cooking time.

Spit Barbecued Large Chicken or Capon

Follow directions for Spit Barbecuing Chicken (page 40). When barbecuing a large 4 to 6 pound fryer roaster chicken or capon, increase barbecuing time to 2¼ to 2¾ hours if unstuffed, 2½ to 3½ hours, if stuffed.

Chicken Pieces or Quarters

Barbecued Chicken Halves or Quarters I

2 ready-to-cook broiler fryer chickens (2 to 2½ pounds), split in half lengthwise or cut into quarters
Melted butter or margarine
2 teaspoons salt
Barbecue Sauce (see page 56), if desired

Remove neck and back bone from chickens so they will remain flat on grill. Rinse pieces; pat dry with paper toweling. Brush each piece with butter or margarine; sprinkle with salt. Arrange pieces, skin side up on **MEDIUM** hibachi or grill 5 to 7 inches from heat. Cook slowly until underside is well browned, 20 to 25 minutes. Brush skin with butter or margarine; turn and barbecue until skin is well browned, about 20 minutes. Brush chicken with melted butter or margarine. Continue barbecuing until chicken is fork tender, about 10 minutes turning pieces once more. Serve plain or with favorite barbecue sauce. Yield: 4 servings.

No-Watch Roasted Chicken Pieces or Quarters

See photo at left

Brush chicken pieces generously with cooking oil, melted butter or margarine. Season with salt and pepper. Arrange in well-greased flat spit basket; clamp on cover and run spit through basket. Attach to spit motor as manufacturer of equipment suggests. Start motor and cook over **MEDIUM** to **MEDIUM-HIGH** heat (375°F.) at spit level until well browned and fork tender, 30 to 50 minutes, depending upon size of pieces. Stop motor; baste every 15 minutes with oil or melted butter or margarine.

Variations

Prepare as for Barbecued Chicken Halves Or Quarters I and change as follows:

MARINATED CHICKEN HALVES OR QUARTERS II: Arrange chicken pieces in large flat dish. Pour Italian Marinade (see page 59) over chicken; turn pieces. Cover; refrigerate 2 to 4 hours, turning pieces 2 or 3 times. Drain; save marinade for basting while barbecuing, if desired. Serve with Barbecue Sauce (see page 56). Yield: 4 servings.

BARBECUED FRUITY CHICKEN: Arrange chicken pieces in large flat dish. Pour Pineapple Wine or Sherry Orange Marinade (see page 59) over chicken; turn pieces. Cover; refrigerate 2 to 4 hours turning pieces 2 to 3 times. Drain; save marinade for basting while broiling, if desired. Serve with Pineapple Barbecue Sauce or Orange Sauce With Cointreau (see page 56). Yield: 4 servings.

BARBECUED ORIENTAL CHICKEN: Prepare as for Barbecued Chicken Halves Or Quarters I (page 41) except substitute Chinese (see page 59) for Italian Marinade and Oriental Dipping Sauce (see page 56) for Barbecue Sauce. Yield: 4 servings.

GRILLED CHICKEN WITH MUSTARD HONEY SAUCE: Brush chicken pieces with Mustard Honey Sauce (see page 56) during last 10 minutes of broiling. Serve with additional sauce. Yield: 4 servings.

BARBECUED CHICKEN PIECES: Select a 2½ to 4 pound ready-to-cook broiler fryer chicken; cut into serving pieces. Prepare as directed in recipe for Barbecued Chicken Halves Or Quarters I (see page 41) arranging pieces in a well-greased hinged broiler or basket before placing on grill; it makes turning of chicken pieces easier. Yield: 3 to 4 servings.

Rock Cornish Hens Spit Barbecued

Gourmet INTERNATIONAL™

See photo at right

4 defrosted frozen rock Cornish hens (¾ to 1¼ pounds each)
1 teaspoon salt
Wild Rice Stuffing (see page 45), optional
⅓ cup melted butter or margarine or a flavored butter spread or basting sauce (see page 57)
Barbecue Sauce (see page 56)

Prepare rock Cornish hens as directed for spit barbecued poultry on page 40. Rub cavity of each hen with ¼ teaspoon salt. If stuffing is used spoon loosely into cavity of each hen using ¾ to 1 cup of stuffing in each. Close cavity, mount on spit as directed for Spit Barbecued Chickens, Tandem-Style, see page 41, using prongs to hold each 2 hens. If preferred, arrange hens crosswise onto spit, one with drumsticks forward, the next with drumsticks backward, etc. This gives you greater capacity but takes a little longer to cook. Brush hens with melted butter or margarine. Attach spit and start motor. Cook over **MEDIUM-HIGH** heat (375°F.) at spit level. See page 40 for way to check temperature at spit level. Place drip pan under spit, if required. Barbecue until hens are tender, 45 minutes to 1¼ hours or until leg joint will move easily. Baste with melted butter or margarine or flavored butter or basting sauce every 10 or 15 minutes. Serve with Barbecue Sauce. Yield: 4 servings.

Broiled Rock Cornish Hens

Gourmet INTERNATIONAL™

Cut defrosted frozen rock Cornish hens in half lengthwise along backbone and down center of breast; remove backbone. Rinse; dry with paper toweling. Skewer wings to body with small metal skewers. Brush with melted butter or margarine or a flavored butter spread or basting sauce (see page 57). Place halves, skin side up, in very well-greased hinged broiler; close. If preferred halves may be placed directly on grill, skin side up. Broil on **MEDIUM** hibachi or grill 4 to 6 inches from heat, turning every 5 to 8 minutes and basting often with melted butter, margarine or flavored butter or sauce. Cook until tender and well browned on both sides, 25 to 30 minutes. Baste with favorite barbecue sauce (see page 56) last few minutes of broiling.

Barbecued Squabs

Gourmet INTERNATIONAL™

Prepare as directed for Broiled Rock Cornish Hens except cover each breastbone with a thick slice of bacon or salt pork and tie securely in place with wings.

Spit Barbecued Duckling

1 fresh or defrosted frozen duckling (4 to 5 pound)
1 teaspoon salt
Stuffing (see page 45), optional
Barbecue or basting sauce (see page 56)

Prepare and mount on spit as directed for spit barbecued poultry on page 40. Attach spit to motor. Start motor; cook over **MEDIUM-HIGH** heat (375°F.) at spit level until drumstick meat is tender, 2 to 2½ hours, 20 to 25 minutes longer if stuffed. Drip pan when used must be emptied when ½ full to prevent flaming. See page 40 for way to check spit level temperature. Baste during last 20 minutes of barbecuing with favorite barbecue or basting sauce. Yield: 3 to 4 servings.

Rock Cornish Hens ▶

Turkeys For Barbecuing

Fresh or defrosted frozen unstuffed turkeys are excellent for spit barbecuing. Turkeys weighing 6 to 12 pounds are available most of the year, 12 to 20 pound ones can be obtained if ordered a few days in advance.

Defrosted frozen boneless turkey rolls weighing 2 to 10 pounds are easy to spit roast and easy to serve. The smaller rolls are usually available, the larger ones can be obtained if ordered a few days ahead.

IMPORTANT! Turkey producers do not recommend that frozen stuffed turkeys be barbecued in outdoor cooking equipment. Cooking must be started when the turkeys are solidly frozen and the cooking takes too long in most cook-out equipment.

How Much Ready-To-Cook Turkey To Buy

TYPE	FOR EACH SERVING ALLOW
UNSTUFFED	
6 to 12 pounds	¾ to 1 pound
13 to 20 pounds	½ to 1 pound
BONELESS TURKEY ROLL	⅓ to ½ pound

To Defrost Frozen Unstuffed or Boneless Turkeys

Follow directions for defrosting on casing or bags or those that follow:

Leave turkey in original casing. Defrost in refrigerator or cold water to cover. Keep water cold by changing it every hour or by keeping pan under cold running water. Count on 1 to 2 days to defrost 8 to 12 pound turkeys in refrigerator, 2 to 3 days for 12 to 20 pound ones. If defrosted in cold water, count on about 8 to 10 hours for it to soften then finish defrosting in refrigerator.

Important No-No's! Never defrost turkeys at room temperature, never in warm water. Use defrosted turkeys quickly. Never store a defrosted turkey in refrigerator more than 24 hours and never refreeze!

To Stuff or Not to Stuff Turkeys

Turkeys, even small ones, take a long time to roast whether cooked on the spit or in a covered cooker.

Turkey producers recommend these birds be cooked unstuffed to reduce total cooking time.

Stuffing can be cooked separately in a covered heavy duty aluminum foil pan. Place pan on grill, along with the turkey in covered cooker during last 40 to 45 minutes of barbecuing or to one side of grill during the last 40 to 45 minutes of spit barbecuing.

Barbecuing Time For Turkeys (Unstuffed Turkeys)*

FRESH OR DEFROSTED FROZEN READY-TO-COOK (Pounds)	INTERNAL TEMPERATURE (°F.)	APPROXIMATE TOTAL COOK TIME (Hours)
UNSTUFFED		
6 to 8	185	2 to 2¾
8 to 12	185	2½ to 3¾
12 to 16	185	3½ to 4½
BONELESS ROLL		
2 to 5	175	1½ to 2
5 to 10	175	2 to 3½

*For stuffed turkey allow 5 to 8 minutes more per lb.

Barbecued Turkey

Turkey Barbecued In Covered Cooker

See photo at left

Clean and tie turkey as directed for spit barbecued poultry (see page 40). Stuffing turkeys greatly increases cooking time so it is not recommended. Stuffing may be prepared and baked separately in covered aluminum foil pan or package and cooked with the turkey the last 45 minutes of cooking.

Push tip of meat thermometer into thickest portion of thigh muscle away from bone. Place turkey on wire grill over drip pan or on 2 sheets of heavy duty foil large enough to pull up around edges of turkey. Roast over **LOW** heat in covered charcoal kettle or gas cooker with dampers open. Brush with cooking oil or melted butter or margarine. Cover; cook, basting with oil or melted butter or margarine every 30 minutes during last 2 hours. Add coals or increase heat as needed to maintain temperature.

Cut band of skin or string on drumsticks 30 minutes before end of cooking time.

Barbecue until meat reaches an internal temperature of 185°F. and dressing 165°F., if used. See page 40 for checks for doneness.

Spit Barbecued Turkey

Prepare unstuffed turkey as directed in general directions for spit barbecuing on page 40. Place on spit as directed on page 40 except run spit through center of turkey starting at breast and coming out just above tail. Tighten screws with pliers after balancing on spit. A turkey rotary roast rack, which can be attached to the spit, may be used, if preferred.

If meat thermometer is used push tip into thickest part of thigh muscle away from bone.

Attach spit to motor and spit thermometer, if available, to spit. If no spit level thermometer is available, see suggestions for estimating temperature on page 40.

Brush turkey with cooking oil or melted butter or margarine. Start motor; barbecue over **MEDIUM** heat (350°F.) at spit level until turkey is fork tender or meat reaches an internal temperature of 185°F. (and stuffing 165°F., if used).

Baste with barbecue sauce during last 30 minutes of barbecuing, if desired. Cool 20 to 30 minutes before carving.

Spit Barbecued Boneless Turkey Roll

Tie defrosted frozen turkey roll securely 1 inch apart the full length of the roll. Mount on spit as directed on page 40. Attach spit to motor. Barbecue over **MEDIUM** heat (350°F.) at spit level until meat is fork tender and reaches an internal temperature of 175°F. Baste with favorite barbecue sauce during last 20 minutes of roasting, if desired. Cool 15 to 20 minutes before slicing.

Barbecued Turkey Pieces

Cut a small (5 to 6 pound) defrosted turkey into serving pieces. Prepare as for Barbecued Chicken Pieces (see page 42).

Old Fashioned Bread Stuffing

¾ cup butter or margarine
1½ cups diced celery
½ cup diced onion
4 cups ½ inch day-old bread cubes
⅓ to ½ cup warm water or chicken bouillon
1 egg, beaten
2 to 3 teaspoons poultry seasoning
1 teaspoon salt
¼ teaspoon pepper

Melt butter or margarine in large frypan. Add celery and onion; cover and cook over low heat until vegetables are tender, not brown. Add remaining ingredients; toss lightly. Use for stuffing chickens, rock Cornish hens, capon, duck or turkey. Yield: About 4 cups.

APPLE STUFFING: Follow recipe for Old Fashioned Bread Stuffing (this page) and change as follows: Reduce celery to 1 cup, onion and butter or margarine to ¼ cup, poultry seasoning to 1 teaspoon and salt to ½ teaspoon. Omit pepper. Add 2 cups chopped peeled apple and 1 tablespoon sugar to butter mixture; cover. Cook slowly until tender, not brown. Fold in ½ cup seedless raisins. Yield: About 4½ to 5 cups.

Wild Rice Stuffing

Melt ⅓ cup butter or margarine in saucepan; add ¾ cup diced celery and ½ cup sliced green onion; cook slowly until tender, not brown. Add 1 teaspoon salt, 1 can (4 ounces) mushroom pieces, chopped, 2 cups cooked long grain rice, 1 package (4 ounces) wild rice, cooked and drained. Toss lightly. Yield: About 4 cups.

Amount of Stuffing to Make

General rule is to allow about 1 cup of stuffing for each pound of ready-to-cook poultry, or:

STUFFING NEEDED	TO STUFF
4 cups	4 pound chicken, duck, capon, or 4 to 6 rock Cornish hens (¾ to 1¼ pound each)
6 cups	6 pound capon
8 cups	7 to 8 pound turkey
10 to 12 cups	10 to 12 pound turkey
16 cups	16 pound turkey

APPETIZERS

Bacon Appetizers

See photo at right

Wrap any of the following with a half slice of bacon; secure with wooden picks or thread 2 or 3 varieties on 4 or 5 inch skewers. Refrigerate until preparation time. To cook place skewers on hibachi or grill 4 to 5 inches above low burning coals; heat and barbecue until food is hot and bacon is crisp and brown. Baste during barbecuing with favorite butter or basting sauce (see page 57). Turn kabobs carefully 2 or 3 times to brown evenly.

Cooked shrimp
Cooked lobster tail slices (1 inch)
Raw scallops
Sautéed chicken livers
Marinated cooked chicken or turkey cubes
Wiener chunks
Vienna sausages
Precooked cocktail sausages
Fresh or canned pineapple chunks
Kumquats
Brandied prunes
Watermelon pickle
Pickled artichoke hearts
Water chestnuts
Canned mushrooms

Pork Pupus

Brown 1½ pounds of boneless lean pork cubes (1¼ inch) in 1 tablespoon hot shortening in frypan over moderate heat until tender. Pour Kabob Marinade (see page 59) over meat; refrigerate until cooking time. Pour mixture into heavy shallow covered pan; heat on hibachi or grill 4 to 5 inches above low burning charcoal. To serve dip hot pork into Mustard Honey Sauce (see page 56). Yield: 10 to 12 appetizer servings.

Tiny Dolmadoes

See photo at upper left

Prepare your favorite hamburger mixture (see pages 24 to 27). Shape into rolls 1½ inches long and ½ to ¾ inch in diameter; chill. Sauté meat rolls in butter or margarine until meat is cooked through, not brown. Brush meat rolls with Zippy Barbecue Sauce (see page 56) or catsup. Roll in wilted cabbage leaves. To wilt leaves drop fresh cabbage leaves in boiling salted water. Drain well. Wrap each meat roll in small cabbage leaf and thread on 6 inch skewers. Cut strips of aluminum foil ½ inch wider and longer than skewer. Arrange each on a strip of aluminum foil. Bring to serving temperature on hibachi or grill 4 inches above **MEDIUM** heat. Brush with sauce and heat, turning once. Serve with barbecue sauce.

Chinese Appetizer Ribs

See photo at lower left

Place 3 pounds baby spareribs (or regular size ribs cut 3 inches wide) in plastic bag in long flat pan. Add Chinese Marinade (see page 59) to bag and close with tie or string. Marinate in refrigerator 2 to 4 hours turning bag 2 or 3 times. Drain ribs; dry well and save marinade. Arrange ribs on hibachi or grill, 5 to 7 inches from **MEDIUM** heat. Barbecue until meat is tender and free of pink meat, 1 to 1½ hours, turning several times. Baste ribs with reserved marinade as needed during barbecuing. Cut into 1 or 2 rib portions. Ribs can be prepared and barbecued ahead of time on large grill or hibachi and warmed up on cocktail size hibachi at serving time. Serve with Chinese, Pineapple or Sweet-Sour Barbecue Sauce (see page 56). Yield: 6 to 8 appetizer servings.

No-Watch Rotisserie Ribs

Follow recipe for Chinese Appetizer Ribs, above, except place drained ribs cut in 1 or 2 rib portions in a spit basket. Start motor; cook over **MEDIUM** heat until meat is fork tender and ribs are well browned, about 2 hours. When meat shrinks back at end of bones ribs are done.

Barbecued Meat Strips

See photo at left

Cut 1½ pounds partially frozen boneless sirloin steak into strips 6 inches long, 1½ inches wide and ⅛ inch thick. Combine and mix ⅔ cup soy sauce, ¼ cup (packed) brown sugar, ¼ cup dry sherry, 1 tablespoon oil, 1 teaspoon ginger and 1 small clove garlic (minced). Pour over steak; marinate 20 to 30 minutes. Thread meat on 6 to 8 inch bamboo skewers. Barbecue to desired doneness on hibachi or grill 4 inches above low burning charcoal, turning often. Serve hot with favorite barbecue sauce (see page 56). Yield: 12 appetizer or 6 entrée servings.

Beef Satay

Combine 1½ pounds beef tenderloin cubes (1¼ inch) and Chinese Marinade (see page 59); mix. Refrigerate 2 to 4 hours. Drain; save marinade. Thread meat on 4 to 6 inch bamboo skewers; dip into reserved marinade or coconut milk. Barbecue on hibachi or grill 4 inches from low burning charcoal to doneness desired. Baste with additional marinade or coconut milk during broiling. Turn as needed to brown evenly. Serve with Oriental Dipping Sauce (see page 56). Yield: About 8 to 10 appetizer servings.

Oysters on Picks

Sprinkle canned or fresh oysters with minced parsley and salt as desired. Wrap each oyster in a half slice of bacon. Secure with wooden picks. Place on hibachi or grill 4 to 5 inches from **LOW** heat until oysters have cooked and bacon is crisp, 4 to 6 minutes. Turn carefully once or twice during cooking. Baste with Bar-B-Q Basting Sauce (see page 58) if desired.

Shrimp Kabobs

See photo at left

Marinate raw peeled large shrimp in Chinese or Lemon Marinade (see page 59). Alternate 2 shrimp, 2 squares of bacon and 2 small mushrooms on bamboo skewers. Place on hibachi or grill 4 to 5 inches from **MEDIUM** heat and barbecue until shrimp turns pink and bacon cooks, 4 to 6 minutes. Brush with Zippy Barbecue or Sweet-Sour Barbecue Sauce (see page 56) several times while barbecuing. Turn once.

Korean Meat Patties

See photo below

Combine and mix 1 pound ground beef, 1 egg, ¼ cup fine dry bread or cereal crumbs, 2 tablespoons chopped green onion, 1 tablespoon soy sauce, ½ teaspoon each of sugar and salt and 6 to 8 drops hot pepper sauce. Shape into 1½ inch patties. Barbecue on hibachi or grill about 3 inches from **MEDIUM** heat, 5 to 7 minutes to desired doneness, turning once. Serve on picks with Sashimi Sauce or Tangy Horseradish Sauce (see pages 56 and 57). Yield: About 3 dozen.

KOREAN MEAT PATTIES WITH WATER CHESTNUTS: Follow recipe for Korean Meat Patties and shape meat mixture around thin slices of water chestnut.

Scallop Kabob Appetizers

Rinse 1 package (1 pound) defrosted frozen scallops. Combine with ¾ cup drained canned whole mushrooms (4 ounce can), 3 tablespoons each of oil, lemon juice and soy sauce, 2 tablespoons minced parsley, 1 teaspoon minced onion and ½ teaspoon salt. Marinate at room temperature 30 minutes, stirring often. Drain scallops and mushrooms; save marinade. Wrap partially cooked half bacon slices around scallops; thread on short bamboo picks with mushrooms and pineapple chunks. Place on hibachi or grill 4 inches from low burning charcoal; barbecue until scallops are cooked and bacon is lightly browned, about 6 minutes per side. Baste with reserved marinade during barbecuing. Turn once. Yield: About 12 appetizer servings.

Polynesian Kabobs

Combine 1½ pounds boneless lean pork cut in 1½ inch cubes and Kabob Marinade (see page 59) in bowl; mix. Refrigerate 3 to 4 hours. Drain meat; save marinade. Sauté meat cubes until tender In 3 tablespoons hot shortening in heavy frypan over low heat. Drain; refrigerate until time to finish cooking. Thread pork cubes, 1½ inch cubes of fresh pineapple, cantaloupe or honeydew melon and 1 inch green pepper squares on 6 or 8 inch bamboo skewers. Heat and lightly brown kabobs on hibachi or grill 4 inches above low burning charcoal, basting often with reserved marinade. Turn as needed to brown evenly. Serve with Sweet Sour Sauce or Sweet-Sour Barbecue Sauce (see pages 56 and 57). Yield: 6 to 8 servings.

Broiled Mushroom Crab-Wiches

Sauté large (2 or 2½ inch) cleaned stemmed mushroom caps in butter or margarine until tender, not brown. Season with salt. Drain on paper toweling. Put 2 mushroom caps together sandwich-fashion with Crab Filling below. Refrigerate until cooking time. Thread onto 4 to 6 inch metal or bamboo skewers. Place on hibachi or grill 4 inches from **LOW** heat and warm to serving temperature 3 to 5 minutes, turning often.

CRAB FILLING: Combine and mix 1 cup flaked defrosted frozen or canned crabmeat, ½ cup shredded Cheddar Cheese, 1½ tablespoons minced green onion, ½ teaspoon salt and a dash of hot pepper sauce. Yield: About 1½ cups.

Rock Cornish Hen Kabobs

Gourmet INTERNATIONAL

Cut defrosted frozen rock Cornish hens into drumsticks, wings, breasts, etc. Sauté pieces slowly in frypan in butter or margarine over very low heat just until tender, not brown. Season as desired with salt. Refrigerate until cooking time. Thread 2 to 4 pieces of orange chunks and rock Cornish hen pieces onto 5 to 6 inch skewers. Place on hibachi or grill 4 to 6 inches above **MEDIUM** heat until hot and lightly browned. Brush with Curried Orange Sauce (see page 56) while heating.

BREADS

Crusty French Bread in Foil

See photo at right

Cut French bread crosswise into 1 or 1½ inch slices being careful not to cut through bottom crust. Spread cut surfaces generously with soft butter or margarine or one of the butter spreads listed on page 57. Center bread on a double thick square of heavy duty foil large enough to wrap bread into a secure package with a double fold on top and ends. Place to one side of a **MEDIUM** grill, 5 to7 inches above heat until bread is hot, 12 to 18 minutes. Turn loaf often.

Variations

Gourmet INTERNATIONAL

Follow recipe for Crusty French Bread In Foil (above); change as follows:

BLUE CHEESE FRENCH BREAD: Use Blue or Roquefort Cheese Spread (see page 57) instead of butter.

GARLIC OR ONION FRENCH BREAD: Use Garlic or Onion Butter (see page 58) instead of butter.

CRISPY BACON FRENCH BREAD: Use Bacony Butter (see page 57) instead of butter.

HERB FRENCH BREAD: Use Herb or Herb-Onion Butter (see page 58) instead of butter.

ITALIAN BREAD: Use Italian instead of French Bread and Italian Butter (see page 58) instead of butter.

PARMESAN CHEESE FRENCH BREAD: Use Parmesan Onion Butter (see page 58) instead of butter. Sprinkle buttered bread with additional Parmesan cheese and oregano, if desired. Brush crusty surfaces with additional Parmesan Onion Butter before wrapping in foil.

French Bread, Hot Rolls and Buns

TOASTED FRENCH BREAD SQUARES: Cut loaf of French bread in half lengthwise then crosswise into quarters or thirds (to make single servings). Spread cut surfaces lightly with soft Garlic or Herb Butter (see page 58). Arrange in hinged broiler if available, cut surfaces up. Place on **MEDIUM** grill, cut surfaces down, 5 to 7 inches above heat until bread heats and toasts a golden brown, 5 to 10 minutes.

Hot Sliced Dinner Breads In Foil

(White, Rye, Whole Wheat, Black, Egg or Potato Bread) Make bread and butter sandwiches using soft butter or margarine. Restack loaf or the number of slices desired. Center bread on a double thick square of heavy duty foil large enough to wrap bread into a secure package with a double fold on top and ends. Place to one side of a **MEDIUM** grill 5 to 7 inches above heat until bread is hot, 8 to 15 minutes, depending upon number of slices being heated. Turn often.

Variations

Follow recipe for Hot Sliced Dinner Breads (above); change as follows:

CARAWAY RYE BREAD: Use light or dark rye bread; substitute Caraway Butter (see page 58) for butter.

CHEESE BREAD: Use white, egg, potato or rye bread; substitute Cheese or Cheese-Chive Butter (see page 58) for butter. Sprinkle with poppy seed, if desired.

CHEESE-DILL RYE BREAD: Use light or dark rye bread; substitute Cheese-Dill Butter (see page 58) for butter.

HERB BREAD: Use light or dark rye, egg or potato bread; substitute Herb or Herb-Onion Butter (see page 58) for butter.

SWEET BREAD: Use white, whole wheat, egg or potato bread; substitute Orange Marmalade Or Apricot Butter (see page 58) for butter.

Hot Rolls and Buns

Cut baked soft or hard yeast rolls or hamburger or hot dog buns in half; spread cut surfaces with soft butter or margarine or a favorite seasoned butter (see page 57). Wrap 4 to 6 rolls or buns in a foil package; heat as directed for Crusty French Bread (see page 48).

Coffee Cake

Wrap loosely in double thick heavy duty foil. Heat as directed for Crusty French Bread (see page 48).

Toasted Rolls and Buns

See photo at left

Cut baked rolls or buns in half; spread cut surfaces with soft butter or margarine. Place, cut side down, in hinged broiler, if available. Place on **MEDIUM** hibachi or grill, 5 to 7 inches above heat until rolls are hot and bread toasts a golden brown, 5 to 8 minutes.

Sweet Rolls

Wrap 2 to 6 rolls loosely in double thick heavy duty foil. Heat as directed for Crusty French Bread (see page 48).

Brown 'N Serve Rolls

See photo page 49

Biscuits, Cloverleaf, Fan Tan, Parkerhouse Rolls, Etc. Remove rolls from package; brush tops and bottoms with melted butter or margarine. Center on a double thick square of heavy duty foil large enough to wrap around rolls. Seal package with a double fold on top and ends. Place, tops up, to one side of **MEDIUM** hibachi or grill, 5 to 7 inches above heat until rolls have browned on first side 4 to 6 minutes; turn package. Brown rolls on second side and finish heating, 4 to 6 minutes.

Variations

Prepare as directed for Brown 'N Serve Rolls (above); change as follows:

CELERY-CHIVE ROLLS: Sprinkle 1 teaspoon minced chives, ¼ teaspoon celery seed and a dash paprika over tops of rolls just before closing package.

FRUIT NUT ROLLS: Substitute a thin coating of Orange Marmalade Or Apricot Butter (see page 58) for butter. Sprinkle 2 tablespoons chopped pecans over top. Serve with additional Orange Marmalade Or Apricot Butter.

Butter Biscuits

Brush tops and bottoms of 1 package (8 ounces) refrigerated biscuits with soft butter or margarine. Arrange biscuits 2 inches from edge of a double thick 18 inch square of heavy duty foil. Fold foil over biscuits; seal with a double fold on all 3 open edges, leaving space for biscuits to rise. Place to one side of **MEDIUM** hibachi or grill, 6 to 8 inches above heat. Bake 6 to 7 minutes or until biscuits are brown on bottom. Turn package; brown second side and finish baking biscuits, 5 to 7 minutes. Yield: 10 rolls.

Onion or Garlic Biscuits

Follow recipe for Butter Biscuits (above) and use Onion or Garlic Butter (see page 58) instead of butter.

DESSERTS

Make-Ahead Peach or Strawberry Shortcakes

Prepare individual biscuit type shortcakes ahead of time, using favorite shortcake recipe or one on package of prepared biscuit mix. Cool. Cut shortcakes in half into 2 even layers. Spread cut surfaces with softened butter or margarine; reassemble. Wrap each shortcake in a double thick square of heavy duty foil large enough to seal top and ends of package with a double fold. While main course is being served place shortcakes on cool edge of grill, 8 to 10 inches above **LOW** heat; allow to warm, turning once. Open foil; shape it into a serving dish with a rim around the shortcake. Spoon sliced sweetened peaches or strawberries between layers and on top. Serve plain, with whipped cream or soft ice cream.

Toasted Coconut Cake Squares

Cut angel food cake into 2 or 3 inch cubes. Press a cake cube onto tines of a long handled barbecue fork. Coat outside of cake with a mixture of honey and sweetened condensed milk (1 part honey, 2 parts sweetened milk) and roll in flaked coconut. Hold cake square over **MEDIUM** hibachi or grill until coconut toasts and cake is warm, turning often to brown evenly. Transfer cake square to serving plate; top with sliced sweetened peaches or strawberries or a scoop of ice cream and favorite sundae sauce.

Fruit Cobbler

Combine 1 package (12 ounces) frozen sliced peaches and 1 package (10 ounces) frozen red raspberries or 1 package (12 ounces) frozen blueberries, partially defrosted and 3 tablespoons butter or margarine in large (10 inch) heavy frypan with flameproof handle. Cover; place to one side of **MEDIUM** grill, 4 to 6 inches from heat. Bring to a simmer to center of pan. While fruits are heating combine and mix 1½ cups prepared biscuit mix, ¼ cup sugar, 3 tablespoons oil or melted and cooled butter or margarine, and ⅓ cup milk (or enough to make a soft dough). Drop 6 to 8 spoonfuls of dough into hot bubbly fruit. Cover. Pull pan to cool side of grill; cook until dough is done, 12 to 15 minutes. Sprinkle top with cinnamon sugar. Serve plain or topped with whipped cream or ice cream. Yield: 6 to 8 servings.

Elegant Fruited Desserts

Spoon Fruity Dessert Sauce (see page 56) over vanilla ice cream, pound cake à la mode, or ice cream filled meringue shells or cream puffs.

Fruit Dessert Kabobs

Group bowls of 1½ inch banana slices, bite-size chunks of fresh pineapple, watermelon pickle slices, unpeeled red plum halves, peeled orange wedges and Mustard Honey or Curried Orange Sauce (see page 56) around a small hibachi. Let each guest thread an attractive assortment of fruit onto 8 inch bamboo or metal skewers. Brush with Mustard Honey or Curried Orange Sauce. Barbecue over **MEDIUM** grill or hibachi, 4 to 5 inches from heat until bananas are a golden brown and fruit is warm. Turn skewer as needed to brown fruit evenly. Serve with additional sauce, if desired.

Flaming Peaches or Pears

Gourmet INTERNATIONAL™

Just before serving time, heat ¼ cup each of butter or margarine, brown sugar and canned peach or pear syrup in heavy (10 inch) frypan. Place over **MEDIUM** hibachi or grill, 5 to 7 inches from heat until syrup is bubbly, stirring constantly. Add 8 small well-drained peach or pear halves and 8 maraschino cherries. Spoon syrup over fruit until it is well glazed and hot. Move pan to a cooler spot on grill to slow glazing. Pour ¼ cup brandy or cognac over fruit. Touch a lighted match to edge of liquid. Serve plain, on pound cake slices or ice cream when flame dies. Yield: 4 to 6 servings.

Bananas Flambé

Gourmet INTERNATIONAL™

Follow recipe for Flaming Peaches or Pears (above) and change as follows: omit fruit syrup and maraschino cherries and substitute 6 ripe bananas, cut lengthwise, for peaches or pears. Yield: 6 servings.

Fruits Flambé

Gourmet INTERNATIONAL™

Drain 1 can (1 pound) each of peach and pear halves; reserve. Combine and mix ¾ cup currant jelly, ¼ cup light corn syrup, 1 tablespoon vinegar and ⅛ teaspoon cloves in large (10 inch) heavy frying pan. Place on **MEDIUM** hibachi or grill 5 to 7 inches from heat until jelly melts, stirring constantly. Add drained fruit; heat, turning fruit in sauce until warm. Pour ¼ cup orange flavored liqueur over fruit; touch lighted match to edge of liquid. When flame dies spoon fruit and sauce over pound or angel food cake slices. Yield: 6 to 8 servings.

Pears Helene

Gourmet INTERNATIONAL™

Peel fresh pears; core to within ½ inch of bottom. Center each pear on a double thick 10 inch square of heavy duty foil. Fill hole of each pear with 1 or 1½ tablespoons of plain or mint flavored semisweet chocolate bits. Wrap securely so pears will stand upright on grill. Place pears at edge of **MEDIUM** hibachi or grill, 4 to 6 inches from heat, until tender. Serve warm with mint sundae sauce or whipped or soft ice cream.

Grilled Bananas

Combine ¼ cup melted butter or margarine, 1 tablespoon each of lemon or orange juice and honey and dash of salt; mix well. Cut 8 double thick 12 inch squares of heavy duty foil. Center a peeled banana on foil; fold edges of foil up around banana. Brush each banana with an equal amount of butter mixture. Sprinkle each with 2 teaspoons flaked coconut. Fold foil around banana into a secure package. Place, folded side up, on **MEDIUM** hibachi or grill, 4 to 6 inches from heat. Cook until tender, 12 to 15 minutes. Serve hot as dessert or with meat course. Yield: 8 servings.

Pineapple Rum Dessert Kabobs

Combine fresh pineapple and/or honeydew or Casaba melon chunks in plastic leakproof food bag. Add light or dark rum (1 cup rum for each quart of fruit). Close bag with metal tie strip provided in plastic bag box, rubber band or string. Chill 1 to 2 hours. Group small bowls of fruit in rum, brown sugar and small bamboo skewers around a small hibachi. Let each guest spear a piece of fruit, roll it in sugar and hold over **MEDIUM** grill or hibachi until surface of fruit glazes and lightly browns. Cool slightly before eating.

Cinnamon Apple Slices

Slice 4 medium-size washed, peeled and cored cooking apples crosswise into 4 rings each. Cut 8 double thick 8 inch squares of heavy duty foil. Center 2 apple rings on each foil square. Pour ½ teaspoon water into center cavity. Sprinkle slices with 2 teaspoons sugar and a dash each of cloves and cinnamon. Dot with 1 teaspoon butter or margarine; sprinkle 1 teaspoon seedless raisins or chopped nutmeats over apples. Seal package; place folded side up on hibachi or grill about 4 inches above **MEDIUM** heat. Cook until apples are tender, 30 to 40 minutes. Serve hot with pork, ham, beef or poultry. Yield: 8 servings.

Grilled Grapefruit

Cut grapefruit in half crosswise; remove seeds and loosen fruit from membrane. Sprinkle surface with sugar and drizzle a bit of sherry, grenadine syrup or crème de menthe over sugar. Center each grapefruit half on a double thick 12 inch square of heavy duty foil. Wrap loosely but securely with a double fold on top and ends. Place, cut surface up, on **MEDIUM** hibachi or grill, 5 to 7 inches from heat and allow to warm, 10 to 15 minutes.

KABOBS

Kabobs and Skewer Cooking

Roasting foods on skewers, sticks or gleaming swords has been a favorite method of cooking for centuries, perhaps never more popular than now. Kabob or skewer barbecuing is fun and smart hostesses realize a skewer party is a wonderfully easy way to entertain.

Much of the work for a skewer party can be done hours before guests arrive. Foods being used can be cut, marinated, precooked as required; sauces prepared and assembled in serving bowls, covered and refrigerated. At serving time foods, tools and supplies can be quickly arranged around a preheated hibachi or small charcoal or gas grill. If room permits, let guests thread their own food on skewers and cook it to taste.

A Few Tricks Make Kabob Cooking Easy

SKEWERS COME IN MANY SIZES, HAVE MANY USES: Short ones for appetizers—guests can fill and barbecue over a tiny hibachi. Big ones, 10 to 15 inches long, are great for full-meal kabobs and 8 to 10 inch bamboo or metal ones are ideal for easy, elegant fruit or dessert kabobs.

FOOD COMBINATIONS ARE UNLIMITED: Almost any favorite combination of foods can be barbecued on a skewer. Thread foods that cook in the same amount of time onto a skewer; precook or parboil (about ¾ done) the longer cooking foods before threading onto skewer.

SKEWERS: Select twisted or double prong skewers for full-meal kabobs, they keep foods in place during cooking. Avoid heavy skewers or ones with wide blades or sharp cutting edges.

GRILL RACK FOR LARGE SKEWERS: Are great to hold skewers in place and keep foods from resting on the grill surface. If no rack is available 2 bricks on the grill to support both skewer tip and handle will keep foods from touching the grill surface.

SOAK BAMBOO SKEWERS BEFORE USING: Soak in cold water 1 or 2 hours so they will resist charring and burning.

DRAIN FOODS WELL: Before threading onto skewers drain foods and the cooking will be quicker.

Kabob Combinations

TO LOAD SKEWERS: Thread an assortment of foods onto skewers which cook or heat in the same time. Or, thread just one kind of food onto a skewer. Foods being served together can then be done at the same time.

DON'T CROWD FOODS ON SKEWERS: The cooking will be quicker! Leave a space between large pieces of food or separate each piece with a small chunk of fruit, olive, etc., to allow the hot air to circulate.

BASTE WHILE BARBECUING: To keep the foods moist and flavorful. See sauce recipes on pages 56 and 57.

MARINATE FOODS: Many believe foods allowed to marinate 1 or 2 hours before barbecuing have a superior flavor. Others prefer the natural flavor of the foods basted and served with a sauce or butter spread (see recipes page 57) or brushed with melted butter or margarine while barbecuing and seasoned to taste with salt, pepper and condiments at serving time.

To Barbecue Kabobs

See photo at left

Preheat hibachi or grill to **MEDIUM** (350°F.) or **MEDIUM-HIGH** (375°F.) at grill level. If no grill thermometer is available test carefully by holding hand, palm side down, an inch or two above grill. Count 1000-1, 1000-2, 1000-3, etc. If hand is uncomfortably warm at 1000-5 it's **LOW,** 1000-4 it's **MEDIUM**, 1000-3 **MEDIUM-HIGH** and 1000-2 it's **HIGH.** Barbecue foods on skewers on grill or on a rack for skewers, elevated on bricks or held in hand. Turn skewers as needed to cook and brown foods evenly. Barbecue foods to desired degree of doneness.

FOR MORE KABOBS: See dessert kabobs on page 51 and appetizer ones on pages 46 to 48.

Kabob Combinations

Gourmet INTERNATIONAL™

BEEF: Select sirloin, tenderloin, choice grade beef chuck or tenderized round. Cut into 1 to 1¾ inch cubes or strips 6 inches long, 1½ inches wide and ¼ inch thick and marinate, if desired (see page 59). Try these combinations:

Beef cubes (1¼ inch), fresh mushrooms, green pepper squares, bacon wrapped canned potatoes and canned onions. Baste and serve with Southwestern or Zippy Barbecue Sauce (see page 56).

Marinate beef cubes (1½ inch) in Oriental Marinade (see page 59) 1 to 2 hours; drain. Combine with fresh or canned pineapple chunks and bacon wrapped water chestnuts. Baste with leftover marinade. Serve with Oriental Dipping Sauce (see page 56).

Beef cubes (1½ inch), big lemon wedges, 2 ounce defrosted frozen lobster tails and green or red pepper squares. Baste and serve with Lemony Butter Or Basting Sauce (see page 58).

Beef strips woven back and forth on skewers around fresh mushroom caps, canned onions and cherry tomatoes. Baste with melted Italian Butter (see page 58).

HAM AND HAM-LIKE MEATS: Use only fully-cooked boneless or canned ham, smoked pork shoulder butt, Canadian bacon, or canned minced ham or luncheon meat. Cut in 1 to 1½ inch cubes; marinate if desired (see page 59). Try these combinations:

Ham, Canadian bacon or canned luncheon meat cubes, bacon wrapped canned sweet potatoes, large fresh pineapple, cantaloupe or honeydew melon chunks and green or red pepper squares. Baste with slightly melted Orange Marmalade Or Apricot Butter (see page 58). Serve with Sweet-Sour Barbecue Sauce (see page 56).

Ham, smoked pork shoulder butt or canned luncheon meat cubes, canned sweet potato chunks, 2 inch banana slices, pairs of preserved kumquats, black figs, or canned prunes. Baste and serve with Mustard Honey Sauce (see page 56).

Ham or any ham-like meat cubes, cantaloupe or Casaba melon chunks, peeled orange quarters and brown 'n serve rolls. Brush with slightly melted Orange Marmalade Or Apricot Butter (see page 58).

FRESH PORK: Boneless pork shoulder, pork loin or pork tenderloin, cut in ¾ to 1¼ inch cubes. All fresh pork must be thoroughly cooked before eating. Cook pork and go-with foods on separate skewers or sauté pork cubes until lightly browned and tender before threading onto skewers with other foods. When fresh pork cubes are cooked on separate skewers use low heat so the meat will cook tender without excessive browning. Marinate meat before cooking, if desired (see page 59). Try these combinations:

Partially cooked pork cubes, 2 inch parboiled acorn squash squares, green pepper ovals and peeled orange quarters. Baste and serve with Mustard Honey Sauce (see page 56).

Partially cooked pork cubes, melon or pineapple chunks, mushroom caps, green pepper squares and canned water chestnuts. Baste with Curry Butter Or Basting Sauce (see page 58).

Partially cooked pork cubes, bacon wrapped canned potatoes, tomato wedges, green pepper squares and parboiled cauliflowerettes. Baste with melted butter or margarine.

LAMB: Use boneless lamb shoulder cut into 1 to 1½ inch cubes, rolled boneless lamb chops, rib chops (1 or 2 ribs) or loin chops (1 to 1½ inches). Chops and large chunks of lamb should be cooked separately on skewers and go-with foods on others. Try these combinations:

Lamb cubes (1¼ inch), pineapple chunks, bacon wrapped canned sweet potatoes. Baste and serve with slightly melted Orange Marmalade Or Apricot or Sherry Ginger Butter (see page 58).

Lamb chops (1¼ inch), precooked on separate skewers. Bacon wrapped canned potatoes, fresh apple or orange wedges on other skewers. Baste with Curry Butter Or Basting Sauce (see page 58).

Lamb cubes (1 inch), green pepper squares, cherry tomatoes, mushroom caps. Baste with Bar-B-Q Basting or Wine Basting Sauce (see pages 58 and 59).

SAUSAGE: Any fully-cooked or brown 'n serve sausage can be used. This includes wieners or franks, bratwurst, knockwurst, Polish or smoked pork sausage or brown 'n serve or precooked pork sausage links. Try these combinations:

Hot dogs, smoked pork sausage links or knockwurst chunks (cut crosswise into 1½ inch lengths), pineapple, precooked Brussels sprouts and tomato wedges. Baste and serve with Pineapple Barbecue Sauce (see page 56).

Smoked pork sausage or brown 'n serve pork sausage links cut in half crosswise, peeled orange quarters and brown 'n serve rolls. Baste with slightly melted Orange Marmalade Or Apricot Butter (see page 58).

Bratwurst chunks (2 inch), 2 inch chunks corn on cob, canned sweet potatoes and crab apple pickles. Baste with Bar-B-Q Basting Sauce (see page 58).

FISH AND SEAFOOD: Small (2 ounce) lobster tails, large raw or cooked, shelled and deveined shrimps, scallops, or 1¼ inch cubes of lean fish (salmon, swordfish, halibut, etc.) may all be cooked on skewers, separately or combined with other foods. Marinate fish or seafood, if desired (see page 59). Try these combinations:

Swordfish or salmon cubes, lime or lemon wedges, bacon wrapped olive or oyster. Baste with Lemony Butter Or Basting Sauce (see page 58).

Bacon wrapped scallops, small mushrooms, shrimp and lime slices. Baste with Mustard Honey Sauce, Herb or Curry Butter Or Basting Sauce (see pages 56 and 58).

Lobster tails, lemon wedges, tomato wedges and parboiled 2 inch zucchini slices. Baste with melted butter or margarine or Lemony Butter Or Basting Sauce (see page 58).

SALADS

Everyone everywhere loves salad so play it cool when the days get warm. When cooking moves outdoors make a pretty salad to tote to the patio or park and enjoy it with the outdoor cook's great steak, chops or burgers. Here are a few salads ideal for serving at cook-out dinners:

Hot Potato Salad

8 slices bacon, diced
1 cup thinly sliced celery
½ cup chopped onion
4 cups sliced cooked potatoes
⅔ cup water
¼ cup vinegar
2 tablespoons sugar
1 tablespoon flour
1½ teaspoons salt
½ teaspoon dry mustard
½ teaspoon celery seed
2 hard-cooked eggs, coarsely chopped
Chopped parsley

Fry bacon until crisp over **MEDIUM** heat on outdoor grill; drain on paper towel. Save ⅓ cup drippings and pour into large frypan. Add celery and onion; cook slightly. Add potatoes; mix carefully. Combine and mix water, vinegar, sugar, flour, salt, dry mustard and celery seed. Pour over potato mixture; cook until liquid is thickened, stirring carefully. Fold in eggs. Sprinkle crisp bacon and parsley over top. Yield: 6 servings.

Hot Romaine Potato Salad

Follow recipe for Hot Potato Salad (this page) and change as follows:

Reduce potatoes to 3 cups. Increase water to ¾ cup and vinegar to ⅓ cup. Omit eggs. Just before serving fold 6 cups torn washed romaine leaves into hot salad mixture; heat quickly. Serve at once. Yield: 6 servings.

Sour Cream Potato Salad

4 cups sliced chilled cooked potatoes
1 cup sliced celery
½ cup chopped onion
3 hard-cooked eggs, coarsely chopped
1 cup salad dressing or mayonnaise
½ cup dairy sour cream
2 tablespoons lemon juice or vinegar
1 teaspoon prepared mustard
1½ teaspoons salt
¼ teaspoon pepper
¼ teaspoon dill weed

Combine potatoes, celery, onion and eggs in bowl. Combine and mix remaining ingredients. Add dressing to potato mixture; mix carefully. Cover; chill several hours before serving. Yield: 6 to 8 servings.

Pickled Cucumber Slices

2 medium-size cucumbers, washed and thinly sliced
1 medium-size sweet red onion, thinly sliced
1 tablespoon chopped chives
½ cup tarragon or cider vinegar
⅓ cup salad oil
¼ cup sugar
½ teaspoon salt

Arrange alternate layers of cucumber and onion slices in shallow salad bowl. Sprinkle with chives. Combine remaining ingredients; heat to dissolve sugar; cool. Pour over vegetables. Cover and chill until ready to serve. Yield: 6 servings.

Tomatoes, Country-Style

4 medium-size ripe tomatoes, peeled and sliced
⅓ cup sliced green onion
2 tablespoons chopped parsley
1 cup commercial French or Italian dressing

Arrange tomato slices in shallow salad bowl. Sprinkle with onion and parsley. Pour dressing over tomato slices. Cover and chill until ready to serve. Yield: 4 to 6 servings.

Tossed Vegetable Salad

½ medium-size head lettuce
½ head Romaine lettuce
1 small head Boston lettuce
1 small sweet red onion, thinly sliced
1 small cucumber, peeled and thinly sliced
2 medium-size tomatoes, cut into wedges
Favorite French, Italian, Russian or oil and vinegar dressing

Wash and tear lettuce in bite-size pieces; drain well. Place in salad bowl. Cover; chill until ready to serve. Drain off any water in bowl. Arrange onion, cucumber and tomato on top of greens. Add dressing; toss lightly. Yield: 6 to 8 servings.

Watermelon Fruit Bowl

Macaroni Dinner Salad

1 package (7 ounces) elbow macaroni, cooked, drained and chilled
1 to 1½ cups diced Cheddar cheese
1 cup diced fully-cooked ham or luncheon meat or sliced fully-cooked wieners
1 cup thinly sliced celery
½ cup thinly sliced radishes
⅓ cup finely chopped onion
1 cup salad dressing or mayonnaise
1 tablespoon lemon juice
1 tablespoon prepared mustard
1 teaspoon salt

Combine first 6 ingredients in bowl. Combine and mix remaining ingredients. Add to macaroni mixture; mix carefully. Cover; chill several hours before serving. Yield: 8 servings.

Waldorf Salad

3 cups diced unpeeled apple
1 cup halved green grapes or pineapple tidbits
1 cup thinly sliced celery
½ cup coarsely chopped walnuts
½ cup salad dressing or mayonnaise
1 tablespoon sugar
1 teaspoon lemon juice
⅛ teaspoon salt
½ cup whipping cream, whipped

Combine fruit, celery and walnuts in bowl. Combine and mix salad dressing or mayonnaise, sugar, lemon juice and salt. Fold in whipped cream. Add dressing to fruit; mix carefully. Chill until ready to serve. Serve on crisp salad greens. Yield: 6 servings.

Watermelon Fruit Bowl

See photo at left

6 to 8-inch piece watermelon, cut from one end
1 small cantaloupe
1 small honeydew
2 cups pineapple chunks, fresh or canned
2 cups pitted sweet cherries or strawberry halves
Mint sprigs

Cut a thin slice off bottom of watermelon so it will set level. Scoop meat out of melon, to within 2 inches from bottom to form bowl. Remove seeds from melon and cut into bite-size pieces. Cut large scallops around edge of melon bowl; cover and chill. Peel and seed other melons; cut into bite-size pieces. Combine fruits. Place melon on a serving plate with rim. Spoon fruits into bowl. Chill until serving time. Garnish with mint. Yield: 10 to 12 servings.

SAUCES, BUTTERS AND MARINADES

Hot Sauces

BARBECUE SAUCE: Combine 1 cup catsup or chili sauce, ¾ cup water, ¼ cup each of cider vinegar, finely chopped onion and celery, 2 tablespoons each of cooking oil and brown sugar and 2 teaspoons Worcestershire sauce. Simmer gently 8 to 10 minutes. Yield: About 2 cups.

BEARNAISE SAUCE: Combine 3 egg yolks, 2 tablespoons light cream, 1 tablespoon vinegar, ½ teaspoon salt and dash of pepper in top of double boiler over gently simmering water. Whip and beat with small wire whisk or rotary beater until mixture begins to thicken. Add ⅓ cup soft sweet butter, a little at a time, and beat well after each addition. Whip in 2 teaspoons lemon juice; fold in 1 tablespoon chopped parsley and 2 teaspoons chopped green onion. Yield: About 1 cup.

CHINESE BARBECUE SAUCE: Combine and heat ½ cup soy sauce, ⅓ cup honey, 1 tablespoon brown sugar, ½ teaspoon each of salt and curry powder and ¼ teaspoon each of pepper, ginger and garlic salt. Stir in ¼ cup well-drained finely chopped preserved ginger and ½ cup brandy; heat. Yield: About 1⅓ cups.

CURRIED ORANGE SAUCE: Combine ¼ cup sugar, 2 teaspoons cornstarch, ¼ teaspoon curry powder, 1½ teaspoons grated orange rind and ¼ teaspoon salt. Stir in 1 cup orange juice and 1 tablespoon lemon juice. Cook, stirring constantly, until thickened. Yield: About 1 cup.

CURRY SAUCE: Sauté ¼ cup each of finely chopped apple and onion in 3 tablespoons butter or margarine until onion is tender, stirring often. Blend in 3 tablespoons flour and 1 teaspoon salt. Stir in 1 cup each of chicken stock or bouillon and light cream. Cook until thick and smooth, stirring constantly. Mix 1½ teaspoons curry powder, ¼ teaspoon grated lemon rind and 1½ tablespoons water until smooth; stir into sauce. May be made ahead and reheated. Yield: About 2½ cups.

FRUITY DESSERT SAUCE: Drain 1 can (8 ounces) sliced pineapple; save syrup. Quarter pineapple slices. Combine pineapple syrup, ½ cup light corn syrup, 2 tablespoons lemon juice or vinegar, 2 tablespoons cornstarch and ½ teaspoon salt; mix. Cook until thickened and clear, stirring constantly. Fold in pineapple and 1 cup diced mixed fresh fruit (oranges, peaches, cantaloupe and/or sliced strawberries); heat slightly. Yield: About 2½ cups sauce.

MUSTARD BEER SAUCE: Melt 2 tablespoons butter or margarine; stir in ¼ cup flour, ¼ teaspoon salt and 2 drops hot pepper sauce. Cook over low heat until ivory color, stirring constantly. Remove from heat. Add 1 cup hot chicken or beef bouillon slowly, stirring vigorously. Stir in 1½ tablespoons prepared mustard. Cook until thickened, stirring constantly. Add ½ cup beer slowly, beating constantly. Yield: About 1¾ cups.

MUSTARD HONEY SAUCE: Combine and mix ½ cup honey, ¾ cup gingerale, 1 tablespoon cornstarch, ¼ cup prepared mustard and ½ teaspoon prepared horseradish. Cook over low heat until sauce is clear and slightly thickened. Yield: About 1½ cups sauce.

PINEAPPLE BARBECUE SAUCE: Drain 1 can (13¼ ounces) pineapple tidbits; save syrup. Combine pineapple syrup, ¾ cup catsup, ⅓ cup finely chopped onion, ¼ cup each of red wine or cider vinegar and well-drained finely chopped preserved ginger and 3 tablespoons brown sugar. Simmer gently 8 to 10 minutes to blend flavors. Fold in pineapple; heat. Yield: About 2½ cups.

SOUTHWESTERN BARBECUE SAUCE: Combine 1 cup catsup or chili sauce, ⅓ cup butter or margarine, ¼ cup coffee, 3 tablespoons Worcestershire sauce, 1 tablespoon sugar and ¼ teaspoon each of salt and pepper. Simmer 10 to 12 minutes. Yield: About 1½ cups.

SWEET-SOUR BARBECUE SAUCE: Combine ¾ cup each of catsup and apricot preserves or orange marmalade, 2 tablespoons lemon juice or vinegar, 1 teaspoon Worcestershire sauce, ½ teaspoon each of horseradish and salt and ⅛ teaspoon pepper. Heat to simmering stage. Yield: About 1½ cups.

ZIPPY BARBECUE SAUCE: Combine ⅔ cup catsup, ¼ cup water or tomato juice, ⅓ cup each finely chopped onion and diced celery, 1½ tablespoons brown sugar and 2 tablespoons Worcestershire sauce. Simmer gently 12 to 15 minutes. Yield: About 1¼ cups.

ORANGE SAUCE WITH COINTREAU: Combine and mix ¼ cup sugar, 2 teaspoons cornstarch and ¼ teaspoon salt in small saucepan. Stir in 1 cup orange juice. Cook until thickened and clear, stirring constantly. Remove from heat. Stir in ¼ cup Cointreau and 2 teaspoons grated orange rind. Serve warm. Yield: About 1½ cups.

SWEET SOUR SAUCE: Drain 1 can (8½ ounces) crushed pineapple; save syrup. Add water to syrup to make ⅔ cup. Combine in saucepan 1 cup sugar, 2 tablespoons cornstarch and ½ teaspoon salt; mix and stir in ⅔ cup cider vinegar and pineapple syrup. Cook until thickened and clear, stirring constantly. Fold in ½ cup coarsely chopped green pepper and crushed pineapple; heat. Yield: About 2½ cups.

Cold Sauces

CORAL SAUCE: Combine and mix ¾ cup salad dressing or mayonnaise, ¼ cup catsup, 2 tablespoons finely chopped pimiento, 2 teaspoons lemon juice, 1 teaspoon horseradish and ½ teaspoon paprika. Chill. Yield: About 1 cup.

CUCUMBER SAUCE: Fold 1 cup well-drained shredded cucumber, ½ cup dairy sour cream, 1 tablespoon finely chopped green onion, 2 tablespoons lemon juice and ½ teaspoon each of paprika and salt into ¾ cup salad dressing or mayonnaise. Yield: About 2 cups.

ORIENTAL DIPPING SAUCE: Combine and mix ¾ cup soy sauce, ½ cup sherry, ¼ cup finely chopped onion, ½ teaspoon sugar, ¼ teaspoon ginger and ⅛ teaspoon pepper. Stir in ⅓ cup well-drained finely chopped preserved ginger. Let stand 1 to 2 hours before using. Yield: About 1½ cups.

SAUCE CHARCUTIERE: Sauté ½ cup finely chopped onion until tender in 2 tablespoons butter or margarine. Add 1½ cups beef gravy (canned or left-over), ¼ cup dry white wine, 2 tablespoons lemon juice and 2 teaspoons prepared mustard; heat and stir in ¼ cup well-drained chopped sour pickles. Yield: About 2¼ cups.

SOUR CREAM ONION STEAK SAUCE: Combine and mix 1 cup dairy sour cream, ¼ cup finely chopped green or red onion, 2 tablespoons vinegar and ¼ teaspoon each of horseradish, salt and garlic salt. Yield: About 1¼ cups.

TANGY HORSERADISH SAUCE: Combine and mix 1 cup salad dressing or mayonnaise, ⅓ cup prepared horseradish, 1 tablespoon lemon juice, 2 teaspoons dry mustard and ¼ teaspoon each of monosodium glutamate and salt. Yield: About 1⅓ cups.

CHATEAUBRIAND SAUCE: Combine 1 cup each of beef gravy (canned or left-over) and dry white wine in saucepan. Simmer gently until reduced to 1½ cups. Add ⅓ cup butter or margarine, 2 tablespoons lemon juice, 1 tablespoon finely chopped parsley and salt and pepper to taste. Stir until butter or margarine melts. Yield: About 1¾ cups.

MUSHROOM HERB SAUCE: Sauté ½ pound sliced mushrooms and 2 tablespoons chopped onion in ¼ cup butter or margarine until mushrooms are limp, about 5 minutes. Add ¼ cup butter or margarine, ½ cup beef bouillon, 3 tablespoons minced parsley, ½ teaspoon crushed leaf tarragon, 1 teaspoon Worcestershire sauce and ¼ teaspoon freshly ground pepper. Simmer gently about 5 minutes. If desired, stir in ¼ cup chopped pickled walnuts and heat. Yield: About 1½ cups.

ONION-WINE SAUCE: Sauté ¾ cup finely chopped green or Bermuda onion in 3 tablespoons butter or margarine until tender. Stir in ¾ cup dry white or red wine, 1 tablespoon vinegar and ½ teaspoon salt. Simmer 3 to 4 minutes, stirring often. Add 2 tablespoons finely chopped parsley and ¼ cup butter or margarine; stir until butter or margarine melts. Yield: About 1½ cups.

QUICK SWEET-SOUR SAUCE: Combine in saucepan 1 cup currant jelly, 3 tablespoons cider vinegar, ⅓ cup well-drained chopped preserved ginger and ¼ teaspoon salt. Heat until jelly melts and mixture comes to a boil, stirring constantly. Yield: About 1½ cups.

SASHIMI SAUCE: Combine and mix ½ cup soy sauce, 1 tablespoon prepared horseradish, 1 teaspoon sugar and ½ teaspoon dry mustard. Yield: About ½ cup.

COLD CURRY SAUCE FOR MEATS: Combine and mix ¾ cup salad dressing, ¼ cup catsup, 2 tablespoons well-drained sweet pickle relish, 1½ teaspoons prepared mustard and ½ to 1 teaspoon curry powder, as desired. Yield: About 1¼ cups.

SPEEDY SOUR CREAM B-B-Q SAUCE: Combine and mix 1 cup dairy sour cream, ½ cup commercial barbecue sauce and 1 envelope (1⅜ ounces) dry onion soup mix. Yield: About 1½ cups.

Butter Spreads and Basting Sauces

BUTTER BASE: Cream 1 cup butter or margarine until smooth and spreadable and follow directions given below for sauce desired:

Variations

ANCHOVY BUTTER OR BASTING SAUCE: Stir 8 minced anchovies, 1 tablespoon each of lemon juice and minced parsley, ½ teaspoon salt and ⅛ teaspoon pepper into Butter Base (this page). If desired, heat until butter melts. Yield: About 1 cup.

BACONY BUTTER OR BASTING SAUCE: Stir ½ cup crisp bacon bits, 2 teaspoons minced parsley and ¼ teaspoon liquid smoke into Butter Base (this page). Yield: About 1⅓ cups.

BLUE OR ROQUEFORT CHEESE SPREAD: Fold ½ cup crumbled blue or Roquefort cheese into Butter Base (this page). Yield: About 1⅓ cups.

CAPER BUTTER OR BASTING SAUCE: Stir ¼ cup drained capers, 2 tablespoons lemon juice and ¼ teaspoon paprika into Butter Base (this page). If desired, heat until butter melts. Yield: About 1⅓ cups.

CARAWAY BUTTER OR BASTING SAUCE: Stir 2 tablespoons caraway seed and 2 teaspoons each of minced onion and parsley into Butter Base (page 57). Yield: About 1 cup.

CHEESE BUTTER: Stir 1 cup shredded Cheddar, Swiss or smoky cheese and ¼ teaspoon each of seasoned salt and pepper into Butter Base (page 57). Yield: About 1½ cups.

CHEESE-CHIVE BUTTER: Stir 1 cup shredded Cheddar or smoky cheese, 2 teaspoons each of chopped chives or green onion and minced parsley and ¼ teaspoon each of seasoned salt and pepper into Butter Base (page 57). Yield: About 1½ cups.

CHEESE-DILL BUTTER: Prepare Cheese Butter (this page) and stir in 2 teaspoons dill weed and 1 teaspoon chopped chives or green onion. Yield: About 1½ cups.

CHILI-ONION BUTTER: Sauté ½ cup minced onion in 2 tablespoons butter or margarine until tender. Add 2 tablespoons lemon juice, 1¼ teaspoons chili powder, ¼ teaspoon each of salt and garlic powder and a dash pepper. Bring to a simmer over low heat. Cool. Beat into Butter Base (page 57) a small amount at a time; beat well after each addition. Yield: About 1⅓ cups.

CURRY BUTTER OR BASTING SAUCE: Whip 1 teaspoon curry powder into Butter Base (page 57). Fold in ⅓ cup drained finely chopped chutney or preserved ginger. Yield: About 1¼ cups.

DILL BUTTER OR BASTING SAUCE: Stir 1½ or 2 teaspoons dill weed or seed and ¼ teaspoon onion powder into Butter Base (page 57). Yield: About 1 cup.

GARLIC BUTTER OR BASTING SAUCE: Mash 1 or 2 small garlic cloves in garlic press or finely chop. Blend Butter Base (page 57), garlic, ½ teaspoon marjoram and ¼ teaspoon pepper. Yield: About 1 cup.

GINGERED BUTTER: Stir ¼ cup drained chopped preserved ginger, 2 tablespoons each of preserved ginger syrup and soy sauce and ½ teaspoon each of curry powder and seasoned salt into Butter Base (page 57). Yield: About 1⅓ cups.

HERB BUTTER OR BASTING SAUCE: Stir 2 tablespoons minced parsley, ½ teaspoon garlic salt and 1½ to 2 teaspoons fines herbes blend into Butter Base (page 57) or if preferred substitute ¼ teaspoon each of salt, crushed sage, thyme and dry mustard for fines herbes. Yield: About 1 cup.

HERB-ONION BUTTER OR BASTING SAUCE: Stir ⅓ cup thinly sliced green onion, ¾ teaspoon fines herbes blend, 1¼ teaspoons dry mustard and 2 dashes hot pepper sauce into Butter Base (page 57). If desired, heat just until butter melts. Yield: About 1 cup.

ITALIAN BUTTER: Mash 1 small garlic clove in garlic press or finely chop. Stir garlic, ½ cup shredded Parmesan cheese, 2 teaspoons oregano and 1 tablespoon chopped chives or green onion into Butter Base (page 57). Yield: About 1⅓ cups.

LEMONY BUTTER OR BASTING SAUCE: Blend 3 tablespoons lemon juice, 2 tablespoons minced parsley and ½ teaspoon grated lemon rind into Butter Base (page 57). Yield: About 1¼ cups.

MUSTARD BUTTER OR BASTING SAUCE: Beat 2 teaspoons dry mustard, 1 teaspoon Worcestershire sauce and ½ teaspoon horseradish into Butter Base (page 57). If desired, heat just until butter melts. Yield: About 1 cup.

ONION BUTTER OR BASTING SAUCE: Stir 1 envelope (1⅜ ounces) dry onion soup mix and 1 teaspoon finely chopped parsley into Butter Base (page 57). Warm until butter melts, if desired. Yield: About 1¼ cups.

ORANGE MARMALADE OR APRICOT BUTTER: Whip ⅔ cup thick orange marmalade or apricot preserves and 1 teaspoon grated orange rind into Butter Base (page 57). Yield: About 1⅔ cups.

PARMESAN ONION BUTTER OR BASTING SAUCE: Stir ⅓ cup each of shredded Parmesan cheese and finely chopped onion and 1 teaspoon each of oregano and seasoned salt into Butter Base (page 57). Warm until butter melts, if desired. Yield: About 1½ cups.

SHERRY GINGER BUTTER: Whip ¼ cup each of drained finely chopped preserved ginger, sherry and orange juice and 1 tablespoon each of soy sauce and lemon juice into Butter Base (page 57). Yield: About 1⅔ cups.

ZIPPY MUSTARD BUTTER OR BASTING SAUCE: Beat ¼ cup prepared mustard, ¾ teaspoon horseradish and a dash hot pepper sauce into Butter Base (page 57). Yield: About 1¼ cups.

ALMOND BUTTER SAUCE: Sauté ⅓ cup slivered blanched almonds in 2 tablespoons butter or margarine over low heat until almonds are a light golden color. Add ½ cup butter or margarine and ½ teaspoon salt; heat slowly until butter or margarine melts. Yield: About 1 cup.

BAR-B-Q BASTING SAUCE: Combine and mix ¾ cup catsup, ¼ cup minced onion, ½ teaspoon liquid smoke and 4 drops hot pepper sauce. Yield: About ¾ cup.

BASTING SAUCE FOR BEEF ROAST: Sauté ¼ cup finely chopped green onion in 2 tablespoons butter or margarine over low heat until limp. Add 1 cup tomato juice, 3 tablespoons sugar and ½ teaspoon salt. Mix ¼ cup lemon juice and 2 teaspoons cornstarch; stir into tomato mixture. Cook slowly until thickened slightly, stirring constantly. Yield: About 1⅔ cups.

BUTTER BASTING SAUCE: Combine and mix 1 cup soft butter or margarine, ½ cup each of cider or wine vinegar and catsup, ¼ cup minced onion, 2 tablespoons minced parsley, 1 tablespoon sugar, ½ teaspoon each of salt and basil and 2 dashes hot pepper sauce. Yield: About 2 cups.

WHISKEY BUTTER: Melt ½ cup butter or margarine in small saucepan. Remove from heat and stir in ¼ to ⅓ cup bourbon, Scotch or Irish whiskey. Yield: About ¾ cup.

WINE BASTING SAUCE: Combine and mix ⅔ cup each of cooking oil and dry red wine, 1 tablespoon lemon juice or vinegar, 1 small garlic clove, mashed, ¼ cup finely chopped onion, 1 teaspoon each of oregano, sugar and salt and 3 dashes hot pepper sauce. Yield: About 1½ cups.

To Marinate

The Easy Way

Arrange meat, fish or poultry in a large leakproof plastic food bag in a flat pan or bowl. Add marinade. Close bag tightly with metal tie strip provided with plastic food bags, rubber band or string. Turn bag over once. Refrigerate for time suggested in meat, fish or poultry recipe, turning bag several times.

The Conventional Way

Arrange meat, fish or poultry in flat dish or bowl. Cover with marinade and mix with food. Cover container; refrigerate for time suggested in meat, fish or poultry recipe, turning food in marinade several times.

CHINESE MARINADE: Combine and mix ⅓ cup each of soy sauce, cooking oil, sherry or pineapple juice and lemon juice, 3 tablespoons brown sugar and ½ teaspoon ginger. Use leftover marinade for basting sauce, if desired. Yield: About 1⅓ cups.

HERB GARLIC MARINADE: Combine and mix ⅔ cup each of cooking oil and red wine vinegar, 3 medium-size garlic cloves (minced), 1 teaspoon each of basil, leaf thyme and salt and ½ teaspoon coarse pepper. Use leftover marinade for basting sauce, if desired. Yield: About 1⅓ cups.

ITALIAN MARINADE: Combine and mix ¾ cup each of wine or cider vinegar and cooking or olive oil, ¼ cup finely chopped onion, 1 crushed garlic clove, 1½ teaspoons oregano, ½ teaspoon salt and ¼ teaspoon pepper. Use leftover marinade for basting sauce, if desired. Yield: About 1½ cups.

ORIENTAL MARINADE OR BASTING SAUCE: Combine and mix 1 cup soy sauce, ½ cup sherry, 2 small cloves of garlic, finely chopped, 1½ teaspoons each of ginger and monosodium glutamate. Use leftover marinade for basting sauce, if desired. Yield: About 1½ cups.

LEMON MARINADE: Combine and mix ½ cup lemon juice, ¼ cup each of cider vinegar and oil, 2 tablespoons each of finely chopped onion and parsley, ¾ teaspoon salt and ¼ teaspoon pepper. Use leftover marinade for basting sauce, if desired. Yield: About 1 cup.

PINEAPPLE-WINE MARINADE: Combine and mix 1 cup each of pineapple juice and red wine, ½ cup chopped onion, 1 tablespoon Worcestershire sauce, 1 teaspoon leaf thyme, ½ teaspoon each of salt and rosemary and ¼ teaspoon pepper. Use leftover marinade for basting sauce, if desired. Yield: About 2½ cups.

ORANGE-SHERRY MARINADE: Combine and mix ¾ cup orange juice, ½ cup sweet sherry, ¼ cup each of vinegar or lemon juice and minced parsley, 3 tablespoons honey or sugar, 1 teaspoon each of basil and rosemary and ½ teaspoon salt. Use leftover marinade for basting sauce, if desired. Yield: About 1⅔ cups.

SHERRY SOY MARINADE: Combine and mix ⅓ cup each of dry sherry or sake, soy sauce and cooking oil, 2 tablespoons honey, 1 teaspoon ginger and 1 small clove garlic, thinly sliced. Use leftover marinade for basting sauce, if desired. Yield: About 1 cup.

STEAK MARINADE: Combine 1 cup vinegar (wine, tarragon or cider), ½ cup each of salad oil and sliced onion, 1 teaspoon salt, 2 cloves garlic (thinly sliced), 6 to 8 whole peppercorns, and ¼ teaspoon each of leaf thyme and rosemary. Use leftover marinade for basting sauce, if desired. Yield: About 1¾ cups marinade.

KABOB MARINADE: Combine ⅓ cup each of soy sauce and lemon juice, ¼ cup each of honey and grenadine or water and 1 teaspoon salt. Use leftover marinade for basting sauce, if desired. Yield: About 1 cup.

WINE MARINADE: Follow recipe for Pineapple-Wine Marinade (this page) and substitute white for red wine, omit onion and add ⅓ cup lemon juice and 1 teaspoon grated lemon rind. Use leftover marinade for basting sauce, if desired. Yield: About 2¼ cups.

TARRAGON MARINADE: Combine and mix 1 cup cooking oil, ½ cup dry red wine, ¼ cup each of lemon juice and tarragon vinegar, 2 teaspoons prepared mustard, 1 teaspoon salt, 3 quartered garlic cloves, ⅛ teaspoon pepper and 1 bay leaf. Add 2 small onions, thinly sliced. Use leftover marinade for basting sauce, if desired. Save onion slices to serve with meat. Yield: About 3 cups.

VEGETABLES

Hot Off the Grill Vegetables So Good, So Easy

Favorite dinner vegetables take on an exciting new flavor when cooked on the grill. Some vegetables, such as corn in husks or potatoes, can be cooked on the grill, others require wrapping in heavy duty foil. Here are ways to prepare cook-out favorites.

Fresh Vegetables... Barbecued In Foil

Center 2 or 4 servings of cleaned prepared vegetable in a double thick 10 to 12 inch square of heavy duty foil. Season as desired with salt and pepper. Dot with 2 or 4 teaspoons butter or margarine or favorite butter spread (see pages 57 to 59). Add 2 or 4 teaspoons water. Wrap securely with double fold on top and at ends of package, leaving space for steam expansion. Place to one side of **MEDIUM** grill, 4 to 6 inches from heat. Cook until tender (see chart below for approximate cook time). Turn packages 2 or 3 times during cooking.

Barbecuing Time For Vegetables

VEGETABLE	SIZE OR SHAPE	APPROXIMATE BARBECUING TIME (Min.)
ASPARAGUS	Whole or 2 inch pieces	10 to 20
BEANS Green, Italian, Wax	Whole or 1½ inch pieces	20 to 35
BROCCOLI	Flowerette and stem, 2 inches long	15 to 20
CARROTS	Cut crosswise into ½ inch slices or lengthwise into quarters	30 to 45
CAULIFLOWER	In flowerettes	15 to 20
CORN KERNELS	Corn cut from ears	20 to 25
EGGPLANT	Peel, cut into 1 inch cubes	30 to 40
MUSHROOMS	Whole or sliced	8 to 12
PEAS	Shelled	15 to 25
ZUCCHINI	Same as carrots, above	25 to 30

Whole Fresh Vegetables... Barbecued In Foil

ACORN SQUASH: Wash, dry, cut in half lengthwise; remove seeds. Fill halves with 1 teaspoon brown sugar, 1½ teaspoons butter or margarine and 1 teaspoon water; season with salt and pepper. Wrap securely in double thick 8 to 10 inch square of heavy duty foil with double fold on top and at ends. Place, flat side up, to one side on **MEDIUM** grill, 4 to 6 inches from heat until done, 40 to 60 minutes. Do not turn during baking. Serve plain.

BAKED POTATOES (White, Sweet or Yams): Wash, dry and rub skin with oil, bacon fat, butter or margarine or seasoned butter. Wrap each securely in double thick 8 to 10 inch square of heavy duty foil. Place to one side on **MEDIUM** grill, 4 to 6 inches from heat until done, 45 to 65 minutes. Turn often.

BAKED POTATOES (Herb, Garlic or Onion): Quarter unpeeled washed and dried potatoes lengthwise. Spread all surfaces with Herb, Garlic or Onion Butter (see page 58). Reassemble potato. Wrap and bake as directed for Baked Potatoes above.

CORN ON THE COB: Remove husks and silk. Spread corn generously with butter or margarine; sprinkle with salt and pepper. Wrap separately in double thick heavy duty foil. Place to one side on **MEDIUM** grill, 5 to 7 inches from heat until kernels are done,* 15 to 20 minutes, turning often.

*To test corn for doneness, prick a kernel with tip of knife or fingernail. If done no milky juices will escape from cut.

BACON CORN: Follow above recipe except substitute Bacony Butter (see page 57) for butter or margarine or wrap each ear, round and round, in a slice of bacon before wrapping in foil.

ONIONS, WHOLE: Wash medium-size onions and leave skin on, or remove peeling, as desired. Prepare and bake as directed for Baked Potatoes (this page). Place to one side on **MEDIUM** grill, 5 to 7 inches from heat; cook until fork tender, 40 to 50 minutes, turning often.

FRESH CORN IN HUSKS: Fold back husks carefully; remove silk. Brush ear with melted butter or margarine. Fold husks back in place. Tie husks at tip end with heavy string. Place to one side on **MEDIUM-HIGH** grill, 5 to 7 inches from heat until kernels are done, 20 to 25 minutes, turning often.

If preferred . . . Proceed as directed above except omit butter or margarine and soak tied ears in cold water 30 minutes before cooking. Drain ears well and cook as directed above.

Frozen Vegetables... Barbecued In Foil

Thaw 9 or 10 ounce packages of vegetables (not creamed or in plastic bag) until they can be broken apart. Transfer vegetables to center of double thick 10 to 12 inch square of heavy duty foil. Prepare as for Fresh Vegetables Barbecued in Foil (page 60), except omit water called for. Cook until tender, 35 to 45 minutes.

Artichoke Hearts	*Corn Kernels*
Asparagus	*Peas*
Beans, Green, Italian or Wax	*Peas and Carrots*
	Snow Peas
Broccoli	*Squash*

Frozen Potatoes Barbecued In Foil

FRENCH FRIES: Spread center of a double thick 8 to 10 inch square of heavy duty foil with ½ teaspoon butter or margarine. Center 1 serving of potatoes on foil. Dot top with ½ teaspoon butter or margarine. Repeat for as many servings as desired. Season with salt and pepper. Close securely. Place to one side of **MEDIUM** grill, 4 to 5 inches from heat until piping hot, 15 to 20 minutes. Turn once.

FROZEN POTATO PUFFS, PATTIES, HASH BROWNS: Proceed as directed for French Fries, above, except cook time will be longer, 15 to 25 minutes.

Cheesy Potatoes

Combine 1 can (10¾ ounces) condensed Cheddar cheese soup and ½ cup milk; stir until smooth. Prepare 4 cups thinly sliced cooked or canned potatoes, ⅔ cup thinly sliced onion and ½ cup each of shredded Cheddar cheese and crisp bacon bits. Alternate layers of potatoes, onion, soup, cheese and bacon bits in 6 or 8 cup foil baking pan. Cover with heavy duty foil crimping it securely to edges of pan. Place on **MEDIUM** grill, 5 to 7 inches from heat until potatoes are hot, 25 to 30 minutes. Yield: 4 to 6 servings.

Fried Potatoes With Bacon

Cut 6 peeled medium-size potatoes and 1 large (2½ inch) onion into ⅛ inch slices. Dice 6 slices bacon. Fry bacon until crisp in heavy frypan on **MEDIUM** grill. Remove bacon pieces from pan; drain. Add potato and onion slices to drippings. Season with salt and pepper. Cover pan; cook until potatoes brown on underside, about 10 minutes. Turn potatoes; sprinkle bacon bits over top; cook until potatoes are browned and tender. Yield: 4 to 6 servings.

Curry Buttered Grilled Potatoes

Melt ⅓ cup butter or margarine in small saucepan. Stir in 1 teaspoon curry powder, ½ teaspoon salt and ⅛ teaspoon pepper. Cut 4 medium-size peeled potatoes into ⅛ inch slices. Brush centers of 4 double thick 10 inch squares of heavy duty foil with curry butter. Brush potatoes with remaining butter. Center ¼ of potatoes on each foil square; wrap securely. Place on grill, 5 to 7 inches above **MEDIUM** heat until potatoes are tender, 20 to 25 minutes; turn packages 1 or 2 times. Yield: 4 servings.

Southwest Zucchini Corn

Melt 3 tablespoons butter or margarine in large frypan on **MEDIUM** grill, 4 to 6 inches from heat. Add ½ cup thinly sliced onion; cook until limp, not brown. Stir in 1½ cups thinly sliced zucchini, 2 cans (1 pound each) whole kernel corn (drained) and ⅓ cup chopped green pepper. Cook until zucchini is tender and corn hot, stirring often. Fold in 2 cups thin tomato wedges, 1½ teaspoons salt and 1 teaspoon chili powder or oregano. Heat; sprinkle with minced parsley. Yield: About 7 cups, 6 to 8 servings.

Zucchini and Tomatoes Italian-Style

See photo page 3, lower right

Cut 4 medium-size washed zucchini diagonally into ¼ inch slices. Wash and stem 3 small tomatoes, cut into thin wedges. Center layers of zucchini slices, tomato wedges and 3 tablespoons thinly sliced green onion on a double thick 18 inch square of heavy duty foil. Dot each layer of vegetables with Parmesan Onion, Italian or Herb Butter (see page 58). Wrap foil into secure package, with double folds on top and on ends. Allow space for steam expansion. Place to one side of **MEDIUM** grill, 4 to 6 inches from heat until squash is tender, about 30 minutes; turn package 2 or 3 times. Sprinkle with shredded Parmesan cheese just before serving. Yield: 6 to 8 servings.

Grilled Herb Tomatoes

Cut 6 medium-size washed and stemmed tomatoes in half crosswise. Melt 3 tablespoons butter or margarine. Brush tomato halves with butter or margarine and mix remaining fat with ½ cup fine dry bread or cereal crumbs and ½ teaspoon each of basil, rosemary and salt. Spoon crumbs over tomatoes. Place to one side of **MEDIUM** grill, 5 to 7 inches above heat until warmed through, 6 to 8 minutes. Yield: 6 servings.

Parmesan Broiled Tomatoes

Wash and stem 3 large tomatoes. Cut in half crosswise. Brush with Parmesan Onion Butter (see page 58). Arrange on **MEDIUM** grill, 5 to 7 inches from heat until heated through, 5 to 6 minutes. Yield: 6 servings.

Green Beans In Tomato Shells

Cook 1 package (10 ounces) frozen cut green beans; drain and add 2 tablespoons butter or margarine or Herb Butter (see page 58). Keep warm. Cut a thin slice off top of 4 medium-size tomatoes. Scoop out seeds and pulp. Arrange tomatoes, cut side up, in shallow aluminum foil pan. Sprinkle inside of tomatoes lightly with salt. Add 2 tablespoons water to pan. Cover; place on **MEDIUM** grill, 4 to 6 inches from heat. Cook just until tomatoes are warmed through, not mushy. Fill tomato shells with hot green beans; dot with additional Herb Butter and serve. Yield: 4 servings.

INDEX

Special Offers from LARK

FONDUE BOOK
Over 250 fun recipes illustrated in full color. Great for exotic food fanciers. (Value to 3.95). Yours for only $1.95 plus 2 carton proofs.

COOKOUT PLACEMATS AND NAPKINS
In high-style blue denim. Comes with 4 bandana-style napkins and 4 placemats. (Value to $10.00). Yours for only $3.95 plus 2 carton proofs.

WICKER PICNIC BASKET
Beautifully hand woven by skilled craftsmen. Size; 16″ x 11″ x 7″. Featuring leather strap hinges and easy-carry handle. (Value to $9.95). Yours for only $5.95 plus 2 carton proofs.

TEAR OFF ALONG LINE

LARK SPECIAL OFFERS: P.O. Box 60-1924, Minneapolis, Minn. 55460

Enclosed are 4 end panels from 2 cartons of LARK King or Filter Extra Long Cigarettes for each item selected with my check or money order payable to LARK Special Offers. Please ship item(s) indicated to address entered below.

☐ FONDUE BOOK
$1.95 plus 4 carton end panels

☐ WICKER PICNIC BASKET
$5.95 plus 4 carton end panels

☐ COOKOUT PLACEMATS AND NAPKINS
$3.95 plus 4 carton end panels

Name: ______________________

Address: ______________________

City: ____________ State: ____________ Zip*: ________

*U.S. Postal Regulations require use of Zip Code. Please include.
Offer void where taxed or restricted by law. Adults only 21 years of age and over.

OFFER EXPIRES OCTOBER 31, 1972

Get All of These Quality Items at Big Savings

LARK—Filter King: 17 mg. "tar," 1.0 mg. nicotine; Filter Extra Long 18 mg. "tar," 1.2 mg. nicotine, av. per cigarette, FTC Report (Aug. '71).